Sermons
for the
Separated

Prof. Donald F. Megnin, Ph.D.

www.trafford.com
North America & international
toll-free: 1 888 232 4444 (USA & Canada)
fax: 812 355 4082

Preface

During World War II, my father had gotten permission from our high school Principal, Mr. Raymond Van Giesen, to have me drop out of high school during the spring plowing and planting season in order to prepare for the annual spring planting on the farm. Subsequently, from the first of March until June first I was allowed to drop out of my classroom to do this necessary work. The letter from Mr. Van Giesen stipulated, however, that I had to return in June in order to take my spring examinations in each of the subjects in which I had been enrolled. If I passed them, I would be able to continue with my class. If I should fail any of them, I would have to repeat those courses in the class behind the one in which I been enrolled.

The reason for the request was due to the fact that my father was a highly trained tool and die maker, trained in Germany, and working during the war in a factory in Syracuse making parts for American tanks. My brother, who had attended the College of Forestry at Syracuse University and had also completed his Second Lieutenancy, was not yet twenty-one years of age. No one could become an officer before age twenty-one at the time and hence he had to work on the farm until August 1, 1942 before he could become a U. S. Army Officer.

I had applied to Syracuse University in 1946 for a degree in psychology and international relations, but had been turned down due to low high school grades. It was not until 1950 that one of my high school friends and his mother informed me that his father had died and left money in his will for me to go to college. I discussed this opportunity with my parents and they both agreed it was too good a gift not to accept. I then sold my cows and machinery to my father and enrolled in the undergraduate program in psychology and international affairs.

Upon graduation from the university I was asked if I would be interested in going to Thailand to teach Thai students for two years. I agreed and from 1954 to 1956 I taught English to Thai students as a Lecturer of English at Chulalongkorn University in Bangkok, Thailand.

After completing my overseas assignment, I worked as an assistant to Dr. Alexander C. Carmichel, minister of the DeWitt Community Church for one year prior to enrolling in the Boston University School of Theology. It was during my second year in seminary that I was recruited to join forty graduate students from across the United States to tour and conduct speeches in the Soviet Union during the first good will exchange program between the two countries in the post World War II era.

Following my two years of working as an assistant to Dr. Howard Thurman, Dean of the Boston University's Marsh Chapel, my wife and I were married in the Chapel and returned to Syracuse, New York as the minister of the First Ward United Methodist Church at 510 Bear Street. It was during this period that I wrote these sermons while attending Graduate School in Syracuse University while working on my doctoral program on a part time basis.

Foreword

These Sermons were prepared some years ago, but they do reflect the nuances of one who is not too sure of where he was likely to go religiously during the course of his fulfillment of religious duties. As the result of a minister who came into the church as the product of contact with a minister who had a great influence on the writer of these sermons, I should like to have the reader understand these sermons are reflective of his own challenges with which he has learned how to cope in coming to grips with an evolving religious outlook which has been growing and changing over many years. These sermons do reflect the author's commitment to the best traditions of the Christian faith as he has perceived them, but who has also spent a considerable amount of time living among people of different faiths.

With these indications reflecting the constant changes and "improvements" in the course of the author's growth and change over several decades, I welcome you to these illustrations of the changes which have taken place 1n the life of the author and which I commend to you to do the same in the course of your lifetime. Do not accept what someone else has proclaimed is the truth, the final thoughts, concerning what should or should not be

Prof. Donald F. Megnin, Ph.D.

included in the litany of faith, but go in search of your own discovery with which you feel comfortable and able to discuss with others without any feelings of shame or hesitation even when confronted by those persons who claim to know better than you what should or should not be accepted as the basis of how to 11ve, work, and believe the formulations of long ago which may no longer hold the "truth" as it was once believed to be central to a person's life.

What Came Out From the Ruin?

In the ancient legends of the Middle East comes the tale of a large bird believed to have lived in either Egypt or Arabia known as the Phoenix. It was peculiar to this bird that it never had more than one existence at any one time and then only as a male. The Phoenix was believed to have lived on the top of a palm tree. It had a life span of anywhere from 500 to 12,000 years. After this long period of time had expired, the Phoenix made a nest of twigs itself out of spice trees and then set fire to it burning itself alive. From out of the ruin of ashes it was believed came another young Phoenix exactly like the previous one, which meant there was never an end to the Phoenix. It lived on into eternity.

The ancient legend might well have been used as something of a parable. It might not have been that these ancient peoples saw something everlastingly true about life. There was simply never a real end to it. It's almost as if the people saw the fact repeatedly happening around them and to them.....Utter destruction, decay, and despair falling upon them again and again, and yet life, like a phoenix, rises from out of the ruin again and again!

When Edward Gibbon, that great British historian, sat amidst the ruins of the Capitol of Rome and fell to contemplating the vanished splendor of the ancient city, he suddenly heard from a neighboring church the strains of the "Magnificat" and when the words reached his ears, "He hath put down the mighty from their seats and hath exalted the humble and meek. Gibbon sprang to his feet and in that moment received the inspiration for his monumental work," The Decline and the Fall of the Roman Empire."

From out of the ruin came the voice of insight affirming once again that time and circumstance may change, and civilizations can outwardly be destroyed. But yet, life goes on!

And Ezekiel wrote, "The cities shall be inhabited and the waste places shall be rebuilt. And the land that was desolate shall be tilled.....the waste and desolate and ruined cities are now inhabited and fortified.....You shall know that I, the Lord, have rebuilt the ruined places!"

I'm sure you've seen an old broken down house that was rebuilt so that it looks bright, like a new one. You would never have thought it was possible before the work was started, but from out of the ruin came a beautiful new house. It's this process of renewal, of seeing the good that can come even from evil that I should like to talk with you this morning. Make no mistake about it.....I am not advocating we must go in search of evil.....It often comes without any help from us.....There are times when we'll feel overwhelmed by it.....Tragedies that will come to us personally.....Experiences that leave us wondering why they ever had to happen to us.....But for that time when evil will inevitably have to be confronted by us, I should like to make the following suggestions:

First, we need to realize the fact that from out of the ruin may come forth a new idea. It may be something we had never thought of before.....Who would ever have thought Germany and France would one day be staunch allies? But today they are and have developed with other European countries such a combination of skills and power that they are fast becoming a great new power in the world! Who would have thought on December 7, 1941 that Japan would one day stand as an ally of the United States whom Japan had just attacked? Who could think of a time in 2016s of the time when the Soviet Union would be dissolved and a host of newly independent nation-states formed? Who would have thought the Peoples Republic of China would one day become a super military and industrial power?

One of the hard facts of our present stiff economic competition with foreign countries is the new equipment and automation systems used by our competitors allowing them to produce more products at less cost. The industrial power of Germany was a shattered shambles at the end of World War II....But today Germany stands in fourth place surpassed only by the United States, China and Japan in industrial production. From out of the total ruin of war have come new industries, cities and scientific techniques which are the fruits of ideas that might not have been had there not been such wholesale destruction.

If it had not been for the tragedy of World War II throwing all parts of the world into social, economic and political upheaval there may not have been felt a real need for the organization uniting all nation-states in the common interest of world peace in the United Nations. Who would have thought that national interests could be brought under the influence of international interests so that the concept of the good of all nation-states is more important than the good of any single nation-state?

On the front cover of Life Magazine some years ago an important announcement was made. For the first time in Japan's long history as a hungry nation-state, it faced the prospect of a nice surplus!

Before World War II, less than thirty percent of the tillable land in Japan was owned by the peasants who worked on it.....They were like serfs working on large estates.....With the defeat of Japan in 1945, American agricultural experts working with American occupation forces initiated radical land reforms which practically took the land away from those who had owned it and gave it to those who had none with negligible compensation paid to the former owners. Incidentally, as much as some Americans are unwilling to hear of it, Fidel Castro did the same in Cuba to which we violently objected. Today, Japan enjoys a standard of living that many western nation-states might envy. From out of the ruin of war came a revolutionary idea that has changed the world!

Secondly, from out of the ruin may come an unparalleled opportunity if it is recognized. In 1666, fire swept over London burning it almost completely to the ground. The whole twisting mass of narrow streets, winding lanes and alleys representing a random chaos of a city, as it had been called, was destroyed. London lay in smoldering ruins. Some people suggested here was an opportunity to create a new city. "Let's not restore that old rabbit-warren. Let's build a new city of London."

That great architectural genius, Sir Christopher Wren, prepared a masterly design for rebuilding London which would have made it one of the most beautiful cities in the world. Wren's design, incidentally, was not very different from the general plan considered almost 300 years later for rebuilding the east end of London so badly damaged by bombs in World War II. Parliament approved the plans. Then the Parliamentarians felt that anything new was a threat to their particular properties. They made haste to restore the old maze! The opportunity to build a beautiful new city cleared of all of its crooked, twisting narrowness was lost. From out of the ruin of the old city an opportunity went unrecognized and lost until the end of the Second World War!

For many years we have stood on the sidelines as various problems erupted around the world. We seemed to be uninterested in what was happening in Africa while our attention was so completely focused on Berlin and the East European countries. We were missing an unparalleled opportunity of advancing our claim that we stood for the unequivocal goal of furthering political self-determination for all peoples, rising the standards of living for humankind with eventual freedom from illiteracy, poverty, disease and crowned by the hope that each person, as a child of God, is endowed with the ultimate right to develop his/her talents to the limits set only by his or her own ability.....This is the cause which should command not only all of our interests, but our wealth, talents and power as well.

We seem to have forgotten the concept of the Kingdom of God.....We cannot continue to pursue such a purpose of limited national interests. In order to meet the challenge of the world's concept of Communism we have always maintained that anything less than a world-wide counter challenge would be less than futile.....It would be inherently limited in both appeal and application. We had to guard against the reactionary tendencies of the John Birch Society and the right-wing of the Republican Tea Party! The Kingdom of God is not only for red-blooded, white pigmented Protestant loyal American Anglo-Saxsons, but we believed it applied to all of the world composed of the infinite variety of peoples and their highly diverse cultures....

Halford Luccock put the nostalgia for the past very abruptly when he gave the illustration of the preacher who said "Our fathers gave us a happy, prosperous country. Instead of keeping it that way we became experts in education, in nutrition, in housing and in welfare." Evidently, in the mind of this preacher, as it wrongly conjured up the light of other days, all of these things are evils. He went on "Think of the years before the era of "experts"; a small town on Sunday, with every thing closed down, everybody in Church, hymns resounding down Main Street and the Sunday dinners. People in those days believed in paying their bills and never thought of getting something for nothing or something that didn't belong to them!"

But then Dr. Luccock really brought this beautiful picture up against the mirror of what these years were really like.....He asked "When was this happy day? In the preacher's youth? In the high days of Warren G. Harding? Perchance the days when people never thought of getting something for nothing!" Or maybe it was back seventy or eighty years ago...in the time that has been called the "age of the dinosaurs" the period of the greatest corruption in American history.....Those were the years trotted out solemnly as the golden age to which we should return! Just get enough hymns floating down Main Street that was closed tight as a drum on Sunday and all will be well!"

The tragedy of this sentimental tripe is that when called by the name of religion it blocks the action of real prophetic faith. Who through faith conquered kingdoms, enforced justice, received promises, stopped the mouths of lions, quenched raging fire, escaped the edge of the sword, won strength out of weakness, became mighty in war, put armies to flight? Perhaps we have faintly picked up the opportunity of these days to advance the universal cause of humankind to gain release from the bondage of oppression, poverty and ignorance.

And finally, from out of the ruin can come new life. An even greater strength can come from having had to go through the experience of ruin.

Historians have pointed out that there were many high minded loyalties in the American colonies who desired to restore the old ties to England after the injustices of taxation were removed. But there was a group known as "the violent men" who said "Let's not restore anything. Let's create something new,"

The new creation, fitted to the destiny of a new continent, began with the Declaration of Independence. From out of the ruin of broken colonial ties came a new, strong, independent nation-state.

There is an inherent wisdom in nature that seems to know what to do when the time to do it has come. Have you ever noticed how a nest of robins is well cared for by its parents? There is the daily search back and forth from the nest to the lawns and fields and back again for a few weeks. But then, the time has come. The young birds are shown how to fly. The parents fly back and forth from the nest to a bush or a limb.The diet of toted bugs, worms and seeds case…..And if the young still do not leave the nest, they are forced out by their parents and as they automatically try their wings, surprise of surprises, they fly! Yet, the way they hung back from the attempt was almost as if to say "We're afraid to leave. We might fall!" And yet, nature had prepared them well for their new life. From out of their nest, a new life awaited them.

Consider, if you will, the umbilical cord.....It is through this cord of vital tissues that the nourishment of food and oxygen pass to the fetus from the mother and the wastes of the child flow out through the mother. This is the vital link sustaining the life of the child within the mother. But after the child is born this vital cord must be cut.....It's usefulness has ended.....A new life awaits the child.

Likewise life may have prepared us for new experiences far greater than any we may have understood. It is sometimes long after the hard, painful circumstances have passed that we can look back and see that new life, new meaning, new purpose was beginning to be born even as we could not see for the tears in our eyes.

On Taking Things For Granted

In Dr. Ralph W. Sockman's book entitled "The Meaning of Suffering" he wrote, "A break in the family circle brings its pang of loneliness, but it may also serve to remind us of the love which flowed so freely through the household that it was taken for granted without gratitude."

He certainly struck a very familiar fact of our existence, didn't he? We seldom realize what we have until we no longer have it. Have you ever noticed how a child will suddenly discover a toy is missing and will search and search for it? If you're an adult or a parent you're quickly called upon to engage in this life and death search until the missing toy is found! You can't rest or sit back because your child won't let you! The toy has to be found even though it may have been taken for granted previously. It's value is greatly enhanced by its loss! The value of what we have sometimes becomes apparent to us only after it's gone. If you've lost a tool or wrench don't you turn the house or garage upside down until you find it? I remember on the farm whenever a wrench dropped out of the tool box located on the tractor, we'd spend literally hours trying to retrace all of the places we had been with the tractor until we'd find the lost wrench. Or if a part came off of a machine, we'd circumnavigate a field any number of times in order to find that particular part. Or if a plane goes down at sea or in the wilderness endless miles are systematically covered until the wreckage is sighted.

The woman in Jesus' parable of the lost coin had ten silver coins which she might have taken pretty much for granted, but when she lost one of them she turned the house upside down until she found it again. And when she found it, she called together her friends and neighbors and said, "Rejoice with me, for I have found the coin which I had lost."

Yes, we take things too easily for granted. We become accustomed to what we like, to what we've read, to what we do and the pattern of behavior our lives follow. So long as nothing bothers us, we don't spend much time or effort in thinking about what our lives would be like without him or her. Just so long as things go along evenly and smoothly that's all we care about....And yet, such a life is an impossible life. We cannot live without strain and stress for God does not let us. He is anxious to see what will become of his children. How they will meet their difficulties. How they will respond in a variety of ultimate confrontations.

What happens when we take things for granted? Or what happens when we become accustomed to having things go our way? Consider these three things that happen when we take these things for granted.

First, we see only part of the picture of life. We dwell in our little worlds; move in little circles; take a lilliputian view of the world. In Jonathan Swift's brilliant and satirical allegory, "Gulliver's Travels" he lives among people who feel their little six inch height gives them the stature and capacity to view the world as it really is for them. But, of course, what they believe their world to be is ludicrous to

Gulliver who knows and sees their tiny world for what it is; mean, small, petty. Their stature is but a measure of their world; small, insignificant, unimportant, except to themselves.

It's exactly the same with us when we take things for granted. We only see a small part of the picture of life. In J. P. Marquand's book, "The Late George Apley" we get a glimpse of a man with a little mind. He only saw part of the picture of life. Friends and relatives had gathered around his deathbed to catch his last words. They expected some great momentous word or words to issue forth. Instead, they heard a solemn whisper, "Do not disturb the rose bushes." He took things for granted except his rose bushes, even at the end of his life.

Have you ever been caught in the midst of some book or story you had to complete by a certain deadline and the electricity went out? Do you remember how you felt? The frustration that built up in you, the anger from being blocked from completing your task? And yet in how many ways are we dependent, really dependent, upon the things we take for granted? Several years ago a violent storm knocked out the electrical power of New York's Manhatten Island for just twelve hours until it was restored. Hospitals had to go on an emergency footing bringing in gas motors to supply the power necessary to operate hundreds of the electrical items from coolers in the labs to the lamps by the patients' beds. Elevators in the skyscrapers no longer operated. Street lights remained off causing traffic snarls the likes of which no one had ever seen. The refrigerators in the restaurants and stores no longer functioned and there was an immediate sell out of manufactured ice. The gas pumps remained idle. The life of a city came to a complete stand-still with the loss of its electric power. One news commentator couldn't help but draw a comparison between this comparatively safe and mild inconvenience with all of its discomfort and even hardship upon the people and asking the question, what would the people have done if it had been an air attack instead of a power failure? He wondered whether we realized how much we took for granted each day in our own limited, little worlds of interest? It's a fair question and one, I admit, all of us should consider when we start taking things for granted!

By taking things for granted, we not only see part of the picture of life, but, secondly, we lose appreciation for human worth. It's very easy to let our "take it for granted" get in the way of our real appreciation for persons. We tend to feel that another person is obligated to serve our ends; to help us fulfill our needs. Many summers ago we saw how really true it was for a person who took service and status so much for granted he couldn't begin to appreciate human worth from anyone who did not fulfill these two requirements for him. It was at a gas station on the edge of the Black Forest that we saw this example. A man drove into the station and bought two marks worth of gas. He noticed a rear tire was rather low. He asked the attendant to check his tire and it turned out to be one-half of a pound different from a previous station where he had also had it checked. He then asked how it was possible to have such a discrepancy and the attendant said, "It really didn't make that much much difference for the tires." The car owner said, "What do you mean? Of course it makes a difference! The tire will wear out much more quickly if the pressure isn't just right!" The attendant tried to explain that even temperature can have an affect upon the tires and cause a change in air pressure or perhaps it was an older tire and the sidewalls were wearing out. The owner of the car, "Nonsense, I just bought that tire last spring!" The attendant was at a loss to try to explain why that tire should be lower. The owner said, "Are you sure your gauge is correct? This unequal balance will make a difference on all of the other tires and cause them to wear out faster!" He continued, "It's this kind of sloppiness that causes accidents."

At this point the station attendant's wife came up and asked what the difficulty was. Her husband told her briefly and she immediately suggested that such a little difference in air pressure in a rear tire was hardly worth worrying about and ridiculed the car owner's fears about safety over such a trivial matter. The car owner's wife had been listening to all of this and when she heard her husband being ridiculed by the station attendant's wife she charged into the fray telling the other woman that such a brash and brazen attitude on her part was entirely uncalled for! And if people such as she produced the tires and gave such crude service at gas stations, it wasn't any wonder there were so many automobile accidents and expensive equipment like cars wearing out so quickly. And with some further parting verbal shots, the car owner drove off obviously feeling fully vindicated by the strong support he had received from his wife and family each of whom had taken it for granted that they had all due respect and service coming to them even though they had lost any appreciation for the worth of this man who honestly was not at fault for their frustration.

Take things for granted long enough and any appreciation you may have had for a person will shrivel and die. Look around you, my friends. Do you see the people who are here week after week? Who carry the burdens of this church? Who teach our children in Sunday School week after week? Who pay our bills? Who handle the organizations of our Church? Put on your suppers, clean up the tables, give us a call to find out if we're coming? Have you lost your appreciation? Have you been taking them for granted?

Finally, by taking things for granted we lose sight of our primary loyalty to God. This is easy to do. We take it for granted that others are going to continue where we leave off. We take it for granted that what we can't accomplish, others will. We take it for granted that if we can't make it to church or to Sunday School or to that work project, someone else will. We take it for granted that if we don't call at the funeral home or if we don't serve on that committee or commission, somebody else will be there. We take it for granted that when our time becomes short or our schedules full it's the Church that can get along without us.We take it for granted that whenever the going gets tough or whenever we don't know where to turn, we can always fall back upon God. We take it for granted that prayer and devotional discipline can always be relied upon for sustenance and support when we need it. Yes, by taking things for granted we can easily lose sight of our primary loyalty to God.

The story is told of Cardinal Richelieu that when he was Prime Minister of France under Louis the X!V, an eminent French surgeon was sent to perform an operation upon the Cardinal. As the surgeon entered, the Cardinal said to him, "You know you must not expect to treat me as you treat those miserable wretches of yours in the hospital." "Your Eminence, " he replied gravely, "Everyone of those miserable wretches, as you are pleased to call them, is a Prime Minister in my eyes!" He took no man for granted no matter what position he occupied, and thus reaffirmed his first loyalty to God.

It was Harry Emerson Fosdick who said it, "A young child does not see that he is undergirded by his country's institutions, unaware even that there is a Constitution of the United States or a Bill of Rights; but later, the national life that has long given him security begins saying to him, I sustained you even though you did not know me." And so it is with us, we take things of character, conduct, truth and love for granted, not knowing what he has done and is doing to undergird and strengthen our lives.

Marching Off The Map

I t was in the late spring of 326 B. C. that Alexander the Great reached the fabled valley of Kashmir with its towering Himalaya mountains border along the Beas river. His great Macedonian army that had followed him and fought for him successfully through eight years of conquest throughout the known world and who were conquerors of the mighty Persian Empire, refused to go any further. For three days the will of the king and people were locked in antagonism. Harold Lamb, in his life of Alexander the Great, states that a wave of consternation had swept through the Greek army when they discovered that they had marched clear off the map!

They had no maps of the region; no charts to indicate what lay ahead; no guide to follow into the unknown. Only the awesome, towering mountains had cast a forbidding silent barrier to further conquests and they refused to go any further.

The late Dr. Halford Luccock, imagining the scene and seeing modern parallels, imagining the scene seeing certain parallels wrote this commentary, "We are conscripted into an expedition beyond landmarks, a thrust outward into new and uncharted territory."

Aren't you caught up by the image of this early experience of mankind? Here they were, they had marched for more than 3,000 miles using rough, crude maps at best, and now they stood on what they thought was the edge of knowledge on the farthest limit of the known world having marched off their primitive Greek maps and desiring to go no farther! while before them lay the splendor of ancient China and India whose civilizations at least matched if not surpassed their own!

We haven't stopped marching yet.....In every realm of life we are marching off the maps of the familiar landmarks; the known guideposts; the clues to certainty and are striking out into ever new and uncharted territories of experience.

In Hebrews 11:8 the verse that epitomizes this restless, searching, thrusting spirit of man striking out into the unknown is still the predominant theme of human life even today as it was then. "By faith Abraham obeyed when he was called to go out to a place which he was to receive as an inheritance; and he went out, not knowing where he was to go."

We are marching off the maps of today into the unknown of tomorrow. More than several decades ago a Russian scientist predicted that atomic energy would be able to remove mountains, construct harbors and melt vast fields of ice. Today there is no longer laughter. but the question of how to prevent radio-active fallout in order to unleash this power for these purposes. In the twenties and thirties, it was quite a thrill for a few daring individuals to take plane rides at county or state fairs. Today, it's becoming increasingly rare to find an individual who has never flown!

Diphtheria, influenza, pneumonia, typhoid fever and smallpox were almost automatic killers once they were contracted. Polio was a definite crippler if not killer even as various cancers and heart disease are still known as the inevitable harvesters of millions of people today. But medical science will one day march off the map in the conquest of these diseases.

In our grade and high school days, it was pronounced with great certainly that no one could survive in space; that it was impossible to live outside of the earth's atmosphere, but the past decades have caused a lot of scientific textbooks to be rewritten. The pronouncement is still occasionally heard that our tiny planet is the only one in the universe that has life on it. And we are but one planet of literally hundreds of millions of known solar systems revolving around a fairly small sized star known to us as the sun. I should hazard the prediction that before this century is out, we shall have discovered not only life on other planets, but perhaps even some far greater examples of organized living than even we have experienced!

We're still marching off maps and there are still a lot more off of which to march! On this first Sunday of the New Year it seems appropriate to exam some of the current maps that set the imitations upon what we will do and how far we will go to push back the unknown. Let us exam some of the maps off of which we should strive to march in this current year.

One of the first maps we should strive to march off this year is the map of narrow interests. It's long been something of a maxim among businessmen, that a business that does not grow dies. If there is no steady advancement even of a small amount, then that business cannot long survive. It has to grow; it has to expand its range of income in order to continue to function as a live business organization. Sales have to exceed costs or else it's a losing proposition. In the business world the measure of success is the margin of profit. If anything interferes with this index, then all other factors are readjusted until this profit is once more obtained.

We are seeking this very process going on today in places like the Congo where representatives of the huge Belgian copper mining industries had negotiated with the central Congo government while Moise Tshombe was running with the remnants of his Katangese government from bush to bush being pursued by United Nations troops. Previously the narrow regional interests of Tshombe and Katanga province suited the profit motive of the huge Union Miniere Company. But with Tshombe obviously no longer holding the reins of power in Katanga the Belgian company marched off the map of the narrow interests of Katanga and on to the broader more inclusive interests of the Congo Republic. Thus their profit interest seemed to continue in harmony with the broader political interests of the Congo Government.

This continual marching off the map of narrow national interests seemed to be going on. In a year's economic round up of business in 1962 Time Magazine stated "Though most businessmen would look back on 1962 with contained enthusiasm, it was a time of significant opening out to the future. It was the year when the world's businessmen became fully aware that in place of many national markets there was emerging a single international market encompassing the whole free world. In 1962 as never before, business strategists made their day to day decisions and long-range plans in the light of the challenges and opportunities of a world market."

The president of France's National Council of Employers, Georges Villiers, said: "Like the Moliere character who spoke prose without knowing it, we are engaging in supranationalism without knowing it. We are engaging in supranationalism without knowing it!"

Both American and European business and government leaders were beginning to recognize that they had to read the map of narrow national interests if they were to survive in this highly complex and interdependent age!

It's no longer possible to live unto ourselves alone either as individuals nor as nations. We have been linked to the rest of the world just as surely as we are to the people of a particular street, neighborhood or city. Hence, what would happen to one person could happen eventually to all persons!

On the Santa Ana Freeway connecting Los Angeles with San Diego a heavy fog settled in on the 27th of December in the early sixties. A woman driver pulled off the freeway partway with a flat tire. This action set off a chain reaction that piled car upon car for over five miles! The toll in this interconnected mishap was: one dead, a mile from the first crash, two critically injured, twenty four in the hospital, twenty five others slightly injured, twenty cars demolished, forty cars disabled and at least two hundred cars involved altogether because one woman pulled partway off the fast freeway to fix a flat tire on a fog bound, slippery freeway. The map of safety always requires marching beyond the limits of narrow interests of one person to the consideration of the many!

The Second map off of which we should march this year is the map of religious bigotry. The day is rapidly coming when religious bigotry will be spoken of as something that happened long ago like the religious massacres that once were a common-place between Catholics and Protestants of the Middle Ages. Bigotry is very subtle. We experience it without even knowing it. There's man whose main pre-occupation is with Catholics and the influence their church wields over their lives. Every time he gets started on this theme he grows increasingly antagonistic. The hierarchy doesn't allow a Catholic to do his own thinking. The Church dictates what an individual's responsibility toward it shall be. The priest is the authority figure who acts on behalf of his bishop and thus sets the conditions of membership within the Church. A Catholic believes a whole series of myths and accepts them for fact. He goes on and on with his recitation until he can no longer find anything whatsoever good to say about a person who is Catholic. He had put this person in a religious pigeonhole with the label of Catholic upon him until he thinks that takes care of the situation. As soon as he hears a person is Catholic, that's it. He feels he had no further responsibility toward him. If you remind this person of his own responsibility toward his church, oh that's a different matter altogether. He doesn't want to be reminded about that. In fact, the mere mention of it, he promptly becomes very quiet until the next time someone mentions something about the Catholic Church and then he's off again on one of his tirades!

There is a movement underway to march off this map of religious bigotry. In Holland in the early sixties, Protestant pastors and Catholic priests exchanged pulpits; Catholic priests attended the consecration of Episcopal Bishops in Dalles and Boston; 150 priests and ministers in St. Louis gathered to discuss reform and reunion. The high point of this movement was the invitation and attendance of non-Catholic observers at the II Vatican Council which until only recently was regarded by Catholics as heretics and schismatics.

This is a new era into which we are entering with our Roman brethren and the friendliness and cordiality of John the XXIII toward non-Catholics is doing a great deal to further the march off the map of religious bigotry and intolerance. Probably the most universal and inclusive a definition of a Christian was one given by the Pope and on what has followed through-out his lifetime when he said, "Anyone who does not call himself a Christian but who really is does so because he does good." Anyone who does good is a Christian. You could not have a broader definition of a Christian than this. It is open to the world!

The final map off of which we should march is the map of faithlessness. This may sound odd to you, because you feel that faith is such a real part of your lives. But it's a kind of faithlessness that says "It won't work!" or "It can't be done!"or "It's simply impossible!" It's the kind of faithlessness that's demonstrated by a person with a severe physical handicap who refuses to do something about it; who believes it is impossible to make any effort because of the strain and pain involved. It is the kind of faithlessness that is summarized by a mother who says about her son, "He's just not college material. He'd never make it!" It's the kind of faithlessness that is found in the remark of a husband who has lost his wife. "What good did religion ever do me? Why didn't God help me when I needed him?"

This is faithlessness. This is the sort of ultimate mistrust that can be immediately seen and heard when the ups and downs of life are tough boy takes; when the hardships seem greatest; when the trials seem more than you can bear. And yet, unless we march off this map of faithlessness we shall continue to dwell in the darkness of our own despair and our futures will be grim and hopeless indeed! What does it mean to march off the map of faithlessness?

Archibald Rutledge, that great naturalist of some years ago once described the impact of what he saw viewing land that had been devastated by a flood which had then receded: "Nature had set about her work of repair..... Everywhere there was an air of severity, as if disaster were temporary....A spirit of subdued triumph brooded over all; a spirit of quiet rejoicing, which kept singing to my heart; "Hope is stronger than fear; love is greater than grief; life is mightier than death; disaster is an incident in time. The shadows and rain of today will nourish the blossoms of tomorrow."

And Abraham, "By faith went out, not knowing where to go." And so, by faith, Columbus persisted in sailing westward.....Luther stood before the Emperor..... Wesley outside the Church of England.....Tom Dooley into the Jungles of Laos and Vietnam.....

The Ashes of Suffering

Dr. Ralph Sockman once wrote of the time several years ago when he was visiting in an upstate city in New York on a bitterly cold winter night when it was ten below zero and the roads were icy. His host's son and his finance had driven over from Cornell some thirty miles away. Before they started back, his host went down to the furnace room and brought a bucket of ashes to put in their car, so that, if they got stuck on a slippery road, the ashes would give the tires some grip. Dr. Sockman then went on to write, "Similarly the ashes of suffering have to be carried on the journey of life so that faith, hope and love can keep going."

You have to carry them with you to give you traction when you again get stuck in a new area of suffering. People try to escape from suffering. They think they can avoid the necessity of it....flee from the reality of it. In Aldous Huxley's book "Brave New World" he pictured a world where all harsh and painful features of life have been removed. The controller says to a recalcitrant man called Savage about this new world, "It's Christianity without tears" Savage relies, "But tears are necessary. You got rid of them. You just abolish the slings and arrows. It's too easy. I don't want comfort. I want God. I want poetry. I want real danger. I want freedom. I want goodness" The controller replied, "You're covering the right to be unhappy." Savage retorted, "All right then, I'm claiming the right to be unhappy!"

Imagine what kind if a world it would be without hardships. Without pain our bodies would have no warning system. Without danger, there would be no adventure in an undertaking. Without friction our cars would not start. Without tears, our eyes could not see nor would they shine.

Suffering is a very vital and necessary part of life. This is not to say, however, that all that happens of evil and hardship to which we are heir is to be viewed as a discipline of us or as a means of bringing forth some purpose of God. So often we find persons who are smug enough to state, that someone else's hardship is a means God has to teach that person a certain kind of lesson. How can you say that when a little child is stricken with polio, or an airplane crashes killing all on board? How can you say that the earthquake which took thousands of lives in Iran last year was an act of God? And yet we hear these things said over and over again. Whenever anything goes wrong very seriously, or we've reached the point where we can find no other explanation...... then we say, oh well, that was an act of God and thereby laying the blame on him and absolve ourselves from all responsibility. But before we consider a few of the values of suffering let us differentiate between the types of evil we find human beings experience. There is first the type called moral evil. Where, due to various choices that individuals have made, some evil, some suffering results. A person who imperils the necessities of his family so that he can have those few extra beers night after night can easily be seen where he contributes to the evil of neglect which we deplore! There is a direct relationship between this person's choices and the results. Or if a person is speeding down the highway and is suddenly confronted with another car stalled on the road ahead and is unable to stop but slams into the other car killing the occupants. We can see where the speed, the act of haste has caused disaster even while disaster was not intended. Suffering was caused by a willful act. Or a boy gets into trouble because his father cared nothing for him. He wouldn't show any concern for his son. He didn't care if he got into trouble. Oh he threatened his son often enough with dire consequences, but he never acted as if he really loved his son. He just let him do what he pleased. He never so much as deprived him of any of his privileges. It's little wonder that the son must suffer from the strictures of the law when his father did not begin to teach him the limits of privilege he would eventually have to learn for himself as an adult. The first type of suffering then results as choice and may be called moral evil, when people determine the evil which results from their day by day choices.

The second type of evil may be called natural evil, or the type over which no individual human being has any control. They would be due to stems, floods, earthquakes, tidal waves, certain types of disease, etc., any evil that has no human will at the root of it. Whenever this natural evil occurs we are speechless, unable to grasp its meaning or understand it's purpose, but yet natural evil of all kinds of suffering can be divided so that you and I or anyone else will experience.

Consider some of the values that can come from suffering. First, suffering can make us humble. It makes it possible for us to learn what another person experiences; what another person goes through. The poet, Oliver

Wendell Holmes, once said he was one who did not take naturally to religion. He felt he had no propensity for religion just as certain persons have no ear for music. But he was turned toward religion "By the discipline of trials in the life of outward circumstance," he had to endure. "It was needful that I should learn the meaning of the text, "Whom the Lord loveth he chasteneth." The force of circumstance can subdue our pride as nothing else can. Consider for a moment what happens when a person has an uncontrollable temper. Think of all of the harm he can do in one of his explosions. The feeling that can be hurt; the joyous attitudes that can be shattered; the affection that can be ruptured; the lives that can be destroyed from an outburst of uncontrollable anger.

Do you remember the story of Moses? How he grew up in the court of the Pharaoh and one day upon an impulse of anger slew an Egyptian who was mistreating an Israelite and hastily buried him in the sand? The next day as Moses was walking along the road he saw two of his Hebrew countrymen in a quarrel. When he criticized "the man that did the wrong," he cried, "Do you mean to kill me as you killed the Egyptian?" Moses then knew that his evil deed of temper had been discovered. He also felt that his own fellow Hebrews were not grateful for what he had done for them. Hence, in dejection and bitterness Moses left Egypt and became a sheep herder in Midian.

It was while dwelling in the exile of his own bitterness of spirit that his people did not understand him; that Moses had an experience of God. It seemed to him that he felt God wished him to return to Egypt and to help his people. From dwelling upon his own pride, self-pity, Moses' spirit became uplifted. He who had withdrawn from those who needed him went back to become their leader in a great exodus from Egypt. The hot temper which had gotten him into trouble as a young man became so disciplined that he led his countrymen for forty years through countless irritations on that grueling trek across the wilderness toward Canaan. And the secret of his patient and persevering leadership was "He endured as seeing him who is invisible." (Heb.11:27) The private suffering of spirit which Moses had borne gave him the humility necessary to become a great leader of his people!

Dr. Sockman raised an excellent question concerning that fact that suffering does not make us humble but can make us bitter as well, when he asks, "When painful misfortune comes, does it humble us or merely humiliate us? If it humbles us, we can find the value in experience. If it humiliates us, we push ourselves further into the morass of suffering through self-pity."

The second value that we find in suffering is that it forces us to outgrow our complacency. Take a look at a child for a moment. Suppose a baby had no interest in moving about; in crawling on the floor; in drawing himself or herself up on his or her wobbly legs.Suppose a child were perfectly satisfied with continually sitting on the floor or staying exactly where you put him or her, happy and content hour by hour with the simple amusements of his/her toys. Suppose the child never wondered about what that intriguing color was on the table. Suppose he/she never tried raising himself/herself and climbing out of the crib. Would you be satisfied with a completely, inert child? Would you be pleased with the fact that your child never tried to walk? Would you feel safe, comfortable, secure in knowing that nothing would happen to your child at all? Of course not! But there are plenty of parents who seem to think this is exactly how they want their children to be! No risks, no fears, no problems, no troubles, no difficulties, no hardships of any kind! But I ask you, how can a child learn to walk, except by suffering a few falls or even many falls for that matter? One grandparent has made the comment, "if there is any absolutely painless way of rearing children, grandparents would surely have discovered it!"

Suffering forces us out of our complacency. We cannot stand still. We cannot control all of the possible dangers we face in life. We cannot rest secure, comfortable and safe in our own little worlds, without destroying the very things we cherish most.

Some years ago, I called in a home where the parents had just told me that their youngest son had not done well in school. The father said "He just won't study. There's too much television and too little study. If a favorite program comes on then off he goes to watch it. He just doesn't spend any thine with his lessons."

I couldn't help but wonder why the boy was doing poorly in school. Where was the parental voice, the authority that said, "Work comes before play? After you've finished your homework you can watch TV?" I could almost see what a supervisor of Public School Teachers meant when he said a few years ago, "The worst thing that could happen to our world would be for our children to grow up to be like us!" I saw happening in the life of this son, what had happened in the life of the father years before. He had not been confronted with the need to outgrow his complacency and spend more time with his studies.

It hurts to grow and sometimes it means that we grow beyond what we originally expected or what others expected. Ask any father or mother how it feels to see their son or daughter leave the home and set up one of their own. I've seen it in home after home. There's a loneliness that nothing can fulfill. There's a gap nothing can ever replace when the boy or girl outgrows the surroundings in which you might have felt he/she was always a part!

The final value that can come from suffering is that we become aware of our dependence upon God. Dr. Peter Bertocci of the Boston University School of Theology in his book "Philosophy of Religion" wrote, "Religion is the faith that God is the ultimate Personal Creator and Sustainer of all values….. Religion is never an escape from suffering and hardship, but it is a fellowship in joy and suffering….. for ends approved by God." Nothing could be more true of the fellowship in joy and suffering which has brought the reality of man's dependence upon God home more completely than the work of men like Gordon Seagrave. He was born in Burma from a long line of missionaries going back three generations. After completing his studies in the United States he returned to Burma using a basketful of instruments that had been thrown out of the operating room at Johns Hopkins Medical School. The operating superintendent decided to clear out all of the useless, broken down surgical instruments that could no longer be repaired. Dr. Seagrave remembering Burma and the instruments that were non-existent asked if he might have the basketful. Hi request was granted and for the next five years these cast-off instruments were used to do all of the surgical work he had to do in his primitive hospital on the Chinese border. Dr, Seagrave was not interested in the fanfare of what he was doing. He simply recognized what needed to be done and did it! The hospital he and his wife inherited when they first went to Burma was a rotting wooden building with twenty bare, wooden beds. The best they could say for it was "If Namkham wasn't what we wanted it to be, we would get off to an early start and do something about it."

And do something about it, they did. Not only did they serve in Burma for almost forty years, but through plagues, epidemics, warfare, poverty, ignorance and as many kinds of diseases imaginable they brought help to the people for whom there had been no help! But for all of the work that Dr. Seagrave and his wife did for the people of northern Burma, nothing surpassed the training of Burmese girls as nurses so that during World War II with their great skill and courage they won the hearts of all who saw them work. These former ignorant, unwashed and by traditional scales of importance, "Lower than male dogs" these girls, "Surmounted their racial and creedal differences for the good of their country, and showed a spirit of selfless, untiring and loving service to the sick and wounded of all races.

Suffering makes us aware that our ultimate dependence is upon God. Dr. Paul Tillick in his book "Shaking the Foundations" wrote, The depth of suffering is the door, to the depth of truth! "Suffering endured with God leads to discovery of life's deeper truths. Pain can be a teacher and purifier. God brings men into deep waters not to drown them, but to cleanse them."

Katherine Mansfield wrote at the end of her long and fatal illness: "What must one do so that suffering can be overcome? One must submit, take it. Be overwhelmed. Accept it fully. Make it part of life. Everything that we really accept undergoes a change. So suffering must become love....I must put my agony into something to change it."

Take the ashes of your suffering with you. You may need them again.

What If They Had Quit?

After Charles A. Lindbergh had flown the Atlantic to Paris, he was brought back to the United States aboard a U. S. Naval vessel. As he watched the seemingly endless expanse of water, he said, "If I had known how big the Atlantic was, I would never have tried it!"

What if Lindbergh hadn't ventured forth across the broad Atlantic? What if he had felt defeated before he started? What if he had quit?

When Albert Schweitzer landed in Gabon with his wife in 1913 and made their way up the Ogowea River to found a hospital for the care of people who had never had any medical treatment of any kind, he found a complete absence of any facilities; a great variety of tropical diseases, and an overwhelming jungle heat day after day. What if he had said, "There are no standards here; no facilities to even act as a shelter from the rain; no one working to help the Africans improve their primitive way of life?" What if he had become bitter because of being interned in a French prison camp during World War I and his abandoned hospital that he had built with his one hands had rotted away through neglect until 1925 when he was able to return? What if he had quit?

It was a long hard struggle through college, med-school and residency for Tom Dooley. When he assisted in the evacuation of Vietnamese refugees from Hanoi after the French defeat at Dienbinphu in 1954, he saw what a mixture of human cruelty and medical neglect can do to ruin the lives of innocent people. What if he had thought what's the use of finishing college and then Med-School on top of that? What if he had said why should I waste my time studying organic chemistry or physical anatomy or the endocrine system? What if the amount of destruction, disease and human indifference had made him say to hell with the whole damn mess? What if he had quit?

When Jesus left his carpenter's trade to begin his ministry he had a hard time getting people to listen to him. They couldn't forget that he was one of them, who had lived and worked just as they had. They knew him as the oldest son of the widow Mary's seven children. What if he had gotten discouraged and said, "People just don't understand what I'm talking about. What's the use of continuing this mission? What if he had decided to go back to his carpentry trade? What if he had decided to withdraw from his ministry? What if he had quit?

What if all of these persons had quit? What if all of the hundreds of thousands of the great men and women in history had said, "What's the use?" And had gone back to their quiet. cozy little corners of the globe resigned to the belief that there was no use doing anything anymore?

We know what the fate of the world would have been if they had decided to quit. We know how impoverished human kind would be if they had quit! And yet whenever we see a great and noble person we see only their accomplishments and forget they had to wrestle with the same inner questioning that everyone goes through about what he/she is doing and why he/she is doing it.

In a conversation I had with a woman many years ago she said, "What's the use? What good did the latin, French, chemistry or geometry ever do me? And the same thing's true about my daughter. Why should she learn all those things and take all of these subjects? She'll never use them! She may just as well quit studying just so long as she passes and graduates. That's all I care about!" And this attitude of defeat, of quitting became as evident in the daughter as it was in her mother! It's not that talent is lacking or that either of them was incapable of accomplishing great things. It's just that there was no incentive left. There was no hope to stimulate their efforts; there was no cause to which they felt they could give themselves. Hence, with no meaning in life, there was no alternative for the future except quitting!

But the persistent, haunting question needs to be asked again and again whenever we feel like giving up spatially and physically. What if they had quit?

I should like to address this issue with you today about the necessity of persistence, of sticking to a difficult task no matter how great the temptation is to leave it. No matter how hard the road is or how long that course of study seems, in order to achieve that distant goal we must continue to pursue it.

One of the first things that should be said about this matter of persistence is that the great achievements of the world have only been wrought through great personal effort and sacrifice. In other words, great results come from equally great efforts. Yes, now and then there's the chance that something great results from very little effort, but don't count on it! I've heard sermons of that variety and you probably have also, where you wondered what the point was the preacher was trying to make. And very likely he didn't really know either. He hadn't given it much thought or effort. While in seminary we used to hear Dr. Howard Thurman speak at the Boston University chapel. Dr. Thurman had a particular style of speaking all his own. He never wrote out his sermons. In fact, it was seldom that he knew from one week to the next what he was going to preach about. But, he could do a brilliant job of preaching without notes or without having written a word previous to the Sunday service. Fortunately, most of the seminarians knew enough not to try to imitate Dr. Thurman! But there were always a few who tried and their voices were controlled and modulated to effect the slow thoughtful speech pattern that he used. The students would take slow hesitating steps and make sudden vivid gestures just like Dr. Thurman did. But that's where the imitation stopped or where it should have stopped because they too appeared not to have written anything previously to the sermon. Their meager, stumbling results, bespoke their neglected efforts.

It was Thomas Edison who said of his inventions and discoveries "It was nine-five percent perspiration and five percent inspiration." There's no worthwhile result without some of the same worthwhile effort put into it first.

Lindbergh was known usually for his great transatlantic flight, but he also worked in developing the first mechanical heart. Dr. Alexis Carrel, the scientist with whom Lindbergh worked spoke very highly of the great personal effort and endurance that he showed throughout their experiences. He said of him in the thirties, "Not only is he very intelligent, but what is very important in achieving success, he is also very obstinate and tenacious, so that he does not admit defeat." The world's great achievements have been wrought through great personal effort and sacrifice. Jan Paderewski, that great Polish pianist and composer thought nothing of going over a single bar of music forty times. Before a concert, he found it absolutely necessary to go through his whole program to refresh his memory.

On one occasion after playing before Queen Victoria she exclaimed with great enthusiasm, "Mr. Paderewski you are a genius!" "Ah, Your Majesty," he replied "Perhaps; but before i was a genius I was a drudge." Without great personal effort great achievements are impossible.

Secondly, we need to realize that an opportunity is only as great as the use that is made of it. I wonder if the people of California realize the sharp controversy that once arose about whether to include them in the territory of the United States, to say nothing of becoming the most populous state in the nation! It was considered a wild desert and only an idiot would think there was any opportunity to be found in California. Daniel Webster, that great and eloquent orator of the U. S. Senate, but one who failed to see any opportunity in that vast area along the Pacific coast, arose in the Senate in 1840 and said, "What do we want with this region of savages and wild beasts, of deserts of shifting sands and whirlwinds of dust, of cactus and prairie dogs? What could we do with the Western Coast of three thousand miles, rockbound, cheerless and uninviting?" I wonder what the Chamber of Commerce of the State of California would say to that today? I'm sure they would say an opportunity is only as great as the use that is made of it and there's no doubt that Californians have made the most of their opportunities.

Take the matter of an education. There are a lot of students who don't begin to realize the use that can be made of it. But it's something great. It can't be quantified exactly. It can't be valued in dollars and cents, although we find most persons view an education in those terms. You can get a better job, you can make more money; you can set your own price. But these are only the incidentals of education. There are not the major values to be obtained from it. If a quality or view of life is not improved then an education has only a market value. It has no greater merit then income production for its holder. An education should stress what a person is, far more than what he has or what he may get. The emphasis has been far too long upon how it can help get what a person hasn't got instead of polishing and brightening what a person already is until it gives forth a brilliance and radiance it might not have had with this additional touch!

I'll never forget what a jeweler once said. "A lot of people seem to think it's the size of the diamond that gives it its value. But that's not true. It's the way it's cur and the type of polish that brings out its real intrinsic beauty and subsequent value.

It's an excellent illustration about what education is meant to do to the intrinsic value a person carries with him into the experience of an encounter with knowledge. The opportunity of education is a rare privilege to bring out the best qualities within a person and to develop what he already has.

And finally, we determine our goals by the methods we use to achieve them. We hear it often said, "The ends justify the means." But don't fall into this trap. It's not true. If that were true, it would mean almost any evil could be employed that would advance our goals. Preventive war could be waged; cruel tyrants could be assassinated; mental defectives could be destroyed before they matured; adultery could produce children for childless couples; the lame, the halt and the blind would be automatically put out of their misery. The aged and infirm would be pointlessly put away. The Nazis tried all of these things assuming the ends justified the means.

That's why we should pity those who fall into the trap of using foul means to reach good ends. It just doesn't work that way. They've already negated their ends and made it impossible to shake lose from the shady effects of their means. Have you ever noticed how many persons make the mistake of thinking that evil doesn't cost anything, but good costs a lot? They seem to feel like Mark Twain's Huckleberry Finn, "What's the use you learning to do right, when it's troublesome to do right and ain't no trouble to do wrong?" Too many people share that idea.....because to do wrong costs nothing in advance; we get what we want at once; paying for it comes afterward. But to do right means paying in advance.....with decision, discipline, devotion, loyalty. Evil, as one preacher put it, may be sold to you on the installment plan.....If a man wants a life of sensual excess he can have that tonight with all of the wild thrill and mad sense of liberation that he seeks now.....but then the bills come in and you pay for it a long long time ever after you've forgotten what you even purchased. It was Harry Emerson Fosdick who said it, "The worst of it is that when the bills do begin coming in for your wrongdoing, they are not all presented to you; those who love you have to pay, those whom you do not really want to hurt, they have to pay!" We determine our goals by the methods we use to reach them. We have to accept the fact that the long term goals of high character, high vocation, and a life of consecrated service must be paid for in advance through the means of self-control, self dedication and self-discipline for these superior ends. We determine our goals by the methods we use to reach them. As a small boy Fritz Kreisler began playing the violin, but with such poor success that he became discouraged. He later tried medicine, painting, and military life in a vain endeavor to find contentment. After years of trying one thing after another, he came back to his first love, the violin. He decided that come what might he would be a violinist and, making up his mind to that, he started with eight solid weeks devoted to finger exercises, and from that point on he practiced the stern discipline that alone could make a great musician possible.

Is there someone here who is anxious to achieve a great and worthwhile goal? Then take heart for you're on your way toward it through the methods you're employing to reach it. What if they had quit? None of us would be here today if they had!

Submerged Hours

According to the Encyclopaedia Britannica, only one ninth of an iceberg is visible and the rest is submerged. How like an iceberg is our own life? So little seen and so much submerged! Whenever we see an outstanding personality or statesman, author, or leader we are apt to feel a great kinship with that person's achievements. We'd like to do that too! Forgetting the untold, endless submerged hours that have been spent by that person in preparing for the achievements that followed.

Do you remember James Thurber's short story entitled, "The Secret Life of Walter Mitty?" Here was a meek, humble hen-picked husband who dreamed his way into becoming a fabulous hero. He sees himself as a great lawyer winning the verdict in the courtroom; a great surgeon taking off his rubber gloves after a successful operation; the eager response of his students to his brilliant lectures as a professor; as a great scientist who has just made an important discovery in his laboratory; as a great businessman gaining a new promotion…..All of the great accolades that come to those who have made a success of translating their submerged hours into great achievements. Yes, all of us see only the high moments and forget the submerged hours that have been invested by those whose accomplishments we applaud!

It's not only the great whose lives are ninety percent submerged, but the lives of each of us as well. What was it the author of Proverbs wrote? "Her lamp does not go out at might. She puts her hands to the distaff, and her hands hold the spineless. She looks well to the ways of her household....." Submerged hours.....spent in an amazingly sacrificial way in order that a few moments of life may be experienced.....may be appreciated by each of us. Without meaning to stoop to the style of extolling the virtues of motherhood for this one day and then promptly forgetting her for the rest of the year, I should like to have us consider how basic parenthood is in submerging untold hours in order that we might be privileged to touch the truly rare and high moments of life in which we feel an overwhelming sense of gratitude for what others have done to make these moments possible. There is little so thrilling as to stand before an alter and exchange vows with the person you've chosen and who has chosen you for life; or to receive a new born son or daughter in your arms; or to stand on a stage and receive a diploma or degree after having gone through the agony, joys, defeats and triumphs of long drawn-out, seemingly endless hours submerged in hardwork, painstaking diligence, perseverance, physical pain, and emotional turmoil before the experience of a lifetime is yours!

The late Halford Luccock once said, "At least three-fourths of any job worth doing well is hack work, routine plugging." Let us consider, then, the essentials of high moments wrought in the submerged hours portrayed so graphically in the lives of our parents. In examining their lives, we find first, that their lives were literally submerged in routine. Their work consisted of a pretty basic routine day after day. Notice, for example, how routinized our lives actually are. Life in the present moments is still a matter of getting up in the morning and going to work.....And the same job perhaps that we had for a long time with the same co-workers; the same building; the same problems. Perhaps it's no longer a matter of splitting wood and starting a fire to cook breakfast, but we still have to get the table set, coffee percolated or hot water boiled .....It's no longer necessary to get the horse harnessed and hitched to the wagon, but we still have to keep the car serviced and in good running order. We may not have to go cross lots to work, but when we get into a five block traffic snarl we must well wish we could.....We may have different means with which to live and work far more comfortably than our parents could ever have dreamed, but we can't avoid the routine of life anymore than they could. We are still submerged in activity. Have you ever tried to imagine what life would be like without routine? Without the knowledge that what we did yesterday will continue tomorrow and the day after? We'd soon find ourselves in emotional chaos. There has to be a certain pattern to our lives that goes on from day to day. Edna St. Vincent Millay recognized it when she wrote, "Life goes on forever, like the gnawing of a mouse, and tomorrow and tomorrow. There's this little street and this little house." It's a recognition that the routine, the repetitiveness is it. "This little street, this little house, this little job is where my life will be played out. Any satisfaction it brings and any contribution it makes will have to be right here."

It's not always easy to accept, is it? But after all of these excursions and experiments have been made there comes the time when the roots of the routine take hold and we recognize the necessity of doing the same thing over and over again.

Do you recall the words you expressed before you accepted a particular position of office or responsibility? You said, "I can't possibly do that. I wouldn't know what to do or say. I'm not smart enough. And then finally you were cajoled into it and through the year you began to discover a dimension within yourself you wouldn't have believed was there. And now in this second year you begin to take things in stride. You've made something of a routine out of it and do what you once never dreamed possible with comparative ease and grace. You find the more you submerge yourself in the routine, the more you experience the high moments as an enjoyable by-product to your task.

The second discovery we make upon examining out parents' lives is that the present is a submerged past. In Luke we find this graphically illustrated in what Jesus said concerning the Kingdom of God. "It is like a grain of mustard seed which a man took and sowed in his garden; and it grew and became a tree, and the birds of the air made nests in its branches. The present is the submerged past that has come to life like a seed that has become a tree!" We sort of take this season of the year pretty much for granted, don't we? We realize the grass needs cutting, the hedges need trimming, the rose bushes clipped and the flower beds spaded and worked a bit, but notice again, the fact that those tulips you planted last year and had almost been written off for dead have blossomed forth in resplendent beauty....The bulbs you planted last year, in the past, are part of the beauty of the present that adds new meaning to this eternal message of spring!

One of the repeated facts that counseling sessions keep bringing up again and again is this of how much present difficulties are the products of a submerged past. Problems of adjustment or personal difficulties may seem very bound up in the present yet they are but the symptoms of a submerged past where they were originally created.

Dr. Floyd L, Ruch in his book "Psychology and Life" wrote concerning the importance of the home, "Home influences probably outweigh the effects of all other environmental impacts combined in determining the fundamental organization of children's social behavior.….. The foundations of children's social attitudes and skills are obviously laid in the home.…..The infant's first experience in trusting and loving other people lies in this process of learning to trust and love his/her parents. The child who experiences anxiety and distrust in this first crucial relationship will tend to have difficulties in meeting social situations, making friends, or forming satisfying marital relationships later. But the child who learns to love and trust his/her parents and to feel secure with them will be more able to form warm affectional bonds with a widening circle of acquaintances as he/she grows up." The present is deeply rooted in the past! We would not exist today were it not for the love, care and concern of our parents yesterday.

The final fact we may recognize from our parents' lives is that the future is submerged in the present. We cannot really understand the future or what may happen in the future unless we can understand what is taking place in the present. This idea is not as strange as it may sound. It's simply an effort to anticipate the future. Recognizing the present is tomorrow's future.

I remember as a little boy I dug into the side hill behind the barn just to see how far I could dig.…..After making an excavation of a few feet deep, I quit.…..It was too much work and besides I tired easily.…..Little boys have a habit of doing things for a while and then dropping them just as they are, unfinished…..There isn't much of a view toward the future in their thinking so that you can literally follow a trail of things partially done…..But look, if you will, at similar scenes where there is this orientation toward the future, If you should be driving up East Adams Street just below the University section you could also see an excavation project. There was a tremendously deep hole thirty to forty feet deep out of which arose a great complex network of structural steel. There were several huge piles of dirt lying about and the mud and dirt were terrific during a rainstorm. And the clouds of dust which were raised seemed to penetrate even closed windows. What a tremendous unfinished piece of what it looks like today! Yet while it was being built we could only see something of its future taking shape in the rough outline of the steel girders being erected…..Emerging from out of this dusty, dirty present was a rising new research and hospital building which houses the headquarters of the Upstate Medical Center which in turn has new medical benefits to give to hundreds of thousands of people throughout this part of the state. Indeed, it has now become part of the experience for some of us to have used these facilities in recent years. And so the future, Indeed, emerges out of the present. This has been true of the past and will ever be true of the present and future. We may express it as symbolically as Martin Luther said when every authority in Germany sought to destroy him, yet he wrote calmly: "Even if I knew that tomorrow the world would go to pieces, I would still plant my apple tree!" Or we may say it as C. F. Andrews said it, that great missionary in India who spoke of it years ago, he looked at his parents and through them came to know and to love Christ. We can trust him because he loved and trusted his parents. His future as a missionary emerged from the ever present example of his parents.

The submerged hours of a person's life are those high moments which are being groomed for eternity.

Old Words With New Meaning: Incarnation

"In a variety of holy books we read how God hath spoken to holy men in many different ways. But hath the present world no sign of them? Is God quite silent in these latter days?"

God is mot silent, we have simply been unable to understand him through the words we still use in religion today. In Dr. Harry Emerson Fosdick's book, "Dear Mr. Brown" he writes: "One of the most dangerous aspects of religion is that it confers sacredness upon everything it deals with. If a certain dome of liturgy has been developed that is sacred, I trust it is not changed. If a certain theological idea has been accepted that is sacred, I trust it to be rethought. If religious thinning has been set in the matrix of an old cosmology, that it is sacred. It is wicked to teach that the earth moves. Perhaps worst of all, this sense of sacredness can attach itself to endless trivialities." We might add, certain words are said which are so ancient and shrouded in mystery we have come to believe them hallowed by the ages and therefore, sacred even though we no longer know what they mean today. They have become part of an ancient legacy we have come to believe should be perpetuated for itself rather than enabling us to understand more of God and the way he acts in the lives of people. Some even go so far as to believe man was made for the words rather than the words for man.

In our Lenten series of old words with new meanings we have considered revelation and found it could mean, disclosure, striking disclosure, a manifestation of God that incarnation could mean a manifestation of potential, an embodiment of a concept or quality, seeing God in human form; that sin could mean behavior contrary to accepted ideals, failure to fulfill our potential, the suppression of truth; that grace could mean an undeserved gift of God, the initiative of God behind life, an obligation to deserve what has been given. Let us consider the fifth old word whose new meaning we seek in this age which calls for a religion which is intelligible, understandable and relevant to our current needs. The old word for the day is salvation. A word that has been historically associated with the doctrine of the new birth. In other words, with the assumption that there is something fundamentally wrong with our lives from which we have to be saved; which we do not have at birth, in fact, this wrongness has been attributed to our birth, as if through our natural birth some particular blemish had been picked up which must be overcome through a new spiritual birth. Don't blame me for this point of view, I'm simply trying to explain the historical view of man's condition as theologians have always stated it. I certainly don't hold to this view myself, but this is what supposedly man has had to be saved from. He's guilty before he even begins, according to this traditional, historical view of the need of salvation for human beings. Other theologians hold that it's not the fact of one's birth from which one needs to be saved, but rather man is enmeshed in a society, in a social order to sin even though it may be unknown to him, from which he must be saved. Again, this is part of the very nature of life into which we are born into a certain environment over which we have no control and, therefore, holds us responsible for conditions we've not created is hardly just! If, on the other hand, we accept life as we find it, as well as ourselves, with a knowledge of our capacities as well as our limitations and the constant source of alternatives ever before us, being neither guilty for a world or conditions we did not create, nor for the alternatives with which we've been confronted. We may examine this old word salvation and see what meaning may yet be garnered from it. If salvation can mean first that we have a constant need for improvement then it may yet have merit and meaning for our days. It's another way of saying, we can never stand still or rest in idle satisfaction with work well done! Isn't this true when we examine the lives of great men and women?

We find as soon as they rest from their labors, as soon as they retire from active participation in the creative outpouring of themselves in life, they not only lose their self-respect, but often their health as well. I'm not suggesting that people shouldn't retire, I'm not suggesting the age limit for retirement shouldn't be dropped. Indeed, very likely it may be radically dropped in this next decade and I would be one of the beneficiaries of this lowered age of retirement. What I am suggesting, however, is taken from the demonstrable facts of some of your lives. You have not used your retirement as an excuse for responsibility, but rather as a new opportunity for other responsibilities and thus you've recognized your own continuing need for self-improvement and self expression!

Contrast for a moment two ministers with entirely different point of view. One is a man who is going to retire in June, the other was retired, but is back in harness again. The first one is counting the days until he finally retires! The other looks forward to several more years of service though he's past seventy five. We can't stand still! Either we are a continuing part of the world's improvement, or we are a part of its dead-weight! I'm being very blunt about this point because I'm interested in having you consider carefully the great temptation of desiring to retire which to the minds of many means not a new opportunity by which to continue their own growth and self-expression, but to increase the leisure of their inactivity. How can there be any self-improvement if a person is not even aware that he or she needs it?

The New Testament is the profound example of an affirmation for the continuing need for improvement in the religious life of a people. Jesus was protesting the religious life of its people.

He was protesting against the hardening of the religious arteries of Judaism where the rites and rules of his faith had become laws unto themselves! He was calling his people to the affirmation of the prophets to love mercy, to do justice and to walk humbly with their God.

Haven't you been shocked by the historical record of our religion which arose as a protest against those who felt there was no need for improving their faith and practices only to find that once this new protest became established as a religion, it also repeatedly resisted the need for continuing improvement and labelled all differences of opinion as heresies?

Salvation can mean a constant need for improvement. There is never an end to what can be done to improve a church, a home, a religion. If we stop using our creative outlets of self-expression, we become like a stream whose source has disappeared and it's only a matter of time until life removes what it can no longer use.

The second meaning that salvation may have is that of searching for more inclusive loyalties. Some weeks ago I received a letter asking whether or not I would be interested in working in a summer camping program with teenagers where the stress would be on helping them to appreciate what is distinctive of being a Methodist. Quite frankly, I couldn't care less. Not about working with teenagers, I really enjoy that, but in helping them to discover what is distinctive of being a Methodist! It sort of reminded me of the little girl who was talking about her religion (she was a Baptist of some sort) as she was talking with her friends one little girl startled her with her comment, Jesus was a Jew. She replied, "Well maybe so, but God is a Baptist! When are we going to overcome these little piddling denominational loyalties that separate us from the love of God? When are we going to learn to respect one another as but a variant of a similar stream? This trend of what's unique about our denomination should begin to be superseded by a consideration of what's unique about our faith, so that this may be superseded by a consideration of what is unique about religion? Our salvation from the evils of divisiveness will come as we recognize the meaning of our salvation in terms of searching for more inclusive loyalties, for larger concepts, for broader references.

We've come a long way, but we still have a long way to go. Dr. William Barclay has written concerning the little loyalties of people, "There are many Church people, it would be a mistake to call them Christian people, who are more concerned with the method of Church government than they are with the worship of God and the service of men. It is all too tragically true that more trouble and strife arises in Churches over legalistic details of procedure than for any other reason."

Look at a man's loyalties and you'll understand a great deal about his character. For whatever a man believes to be important, he will give his time, his energy and his money.

Dr. Edgar S. Brightman in his book, "Moral Laws" wrote "The wider the range of perspective taken into account in establishing ideals and determining conduct, the greater the likelihood of eventual subjective and social consistency and harmony." We might paraphrase to say the narrower the range of outlook in establishing ideals, the greater the likelihood of subjective and social inconsistency and conflict. Hitler did not have a very wide range of perspectives or outlook and his very name epitomizes social conflict!

Several years ago a woman told me how years earlier, when she was twelve years old, her Sunday School teacher wanted her to sign a pledge by which she would promise never to smoke, drink, or play cards, all of the vices of the devil, throughout her lifetime. She said she didn't sign the statement and the teacher was very angry with her. When she told her mother, she agreed she didn't have to sign anything like that.

I was interested in her comment about her teacher. She said, she was mean and cranky. Hardly a person, evidently, who knew what a wide range of perspective was setting up ideals either for herself or her girls that would grow in personal contentment and in her social relationships! Salvation then, may mean a search for ever wider, broader, more inclusive loyalties than those we presently hold.

The final meaning that salvation can have is that of a search for an expressed purpose. It was Friederich Nietzsche who said, "Show me you are redeemed and I will believe in your redeemer." Let us see within ourselves what we profess to believe and then what you say will be clearly understood; salvation will be recognized as the expressed purpose of God in human life!

There was a time in Moslem countries when it was not possible for active preaching and proselytizing to take place on the part of Christian missionaries. If an evangelistic campaign were to be carried out all those foreigners involved in it would be immediately expelled from the country if not executed. In Moslem countries it is no longer possible for active preaching or proselytizing to take place on the part of Christian missionaries. If an evangelistic campaign were to be carried out, all those foreigners involved in it would be immediately expelled from the country and the indigenous Christians restricted in all future gatherings one sabbath service only (if any would be permitted.) The concept of Christian Missionary activity is undergoing a long needed and fundamental change from proclamation to expression, from a profession of faith to a silent witness through service, from a dogmatic rejection of the history and culture of a people, to an open understanding of what their tradition is and how improvements may best be made within that which they already have. It's a light that is seen, a spark that is caught, a life that speaks for itself of the purpose of God through the expression of service rendered by each person in an active brotherhood who works within its borders.

A weaving apprentice was working one day on a loom that his employer had taught him how to use. He kept looking at the ends of the threads and pulling them as he had been taught as the loom worked its wonder upon the interweaving patterns of the rug. He saw nothing but the odd strands of different colored threads as he worked. When his employer returned he suggested that the apprentice stand back some distance from the loom. Only then did the young man discover the beauty of the design upon which he was working. The purpose of his unknown efforts became clear as he saw the expression of it before him.

Why do we engage in worship services? In the weekly rite of coming together for song and praise and the spoken word? Why do we participate in study, in work, in the hundred and one seemingly stray ends of activity which comprise our lives? In order to recognize our needs and the ways they are channeled into life changing ways that change our lives from struggle to hope for the future!

"Old Words With New Meaning: Incarnation"

"In holy books we read how God hath Spoken
To Holy men in many different ways;
But hath the present world no sign or token?
Is God quite silent in these latter days?"

We shall consider again how God is still speaking in these latter days. The question was raised last week following the service of who decides which words have lost their meaning? It's a legitimate question and shows that the person is giving very serious thought to the consequences of this series of sermons during Lent. Another question that might be asked concerning this proposal to review our religious vocabulary is if various practices or words have lost their meaning is this any reason for dropping them?

How can we drop some of these old hymns, for example, that are a part of our tradition?

These are good questions and they really come to the heart of the matter very quickly, but what you do with your religious practices, which words you accept and which ones you reject depends upon what your view of religion is.

If you are a fundamentalist you can't tolerate even an iota of change. They would be heresy for you. If you are a traditionalist, you feel these ancient rites and words must continue because they were part of the tradition of your fathers and therefore, holy to you! To drop them would be a sacrilege.

If you are a naturalist in the theological sense, then you repeatedly test your faith in the light of new experiences arising from related causal factors.

If you are a liberal then you reserve the right to question any precept, examine any truth-claim, evaluate every doctrine in the light of other areas of knowledge and experience and to review the tradition and vocabulary of religion periodically to allow the spirit of the age to speak anew to the heart of human beings.

There is no single word or series of words that can ever fully express truth at any one time, for truth is never total nor complete, but unfolding and fragmentary at any one point in time. And then as new truth is discovered, it is incorporated into the collective body of knowledge with old truths, no longer true or acceptable replaced with newer more complete expression of truth in the present until some newer or more complete expressions of truth in the present come about or until some newer complete expressions of truth in the present or until some newer or even better expressions of it comes along.

Sir Isaac Newton expressed the epitome of humility in the face of continuously unfolding truth when he said of himself and his own great scientific and mathematical discoveries. "I do not know what I may appear to the world, but to myself I seem to have been only like a boy playing on the seashore, and diverting myself in now and then finding a smoother pebble or a prettier shell than ordinary, whilst the great ocean of truth lay all undiscovered before me."

Let us consider, then, the finding of some smoother pebbles or prettier shells of meaning than ordinary from the second old word of our series that needs to have new meaning drawn out of it if its truth is to be seen today and if we are to hear God speak through it in these latter days. The word I've selected for our consideration this week is incarnation. Its footage is in the old Christian doctrine that God became man in Jesus Christ. But so much confusion and difference of opinion exists among different authorities on this point that it's necessary for us to clarify its meaning.

The first meaning that incarnation has is that of the manifestation of potential. I'm sure we've all heard the old cliche, "Nothing ventured nothing gained." But have you ever considered how very true this is? Without trying, without making an effort, without spending ourselves in moving toward a particular goal, no goal is accomplished. The usual expression for this attitude is nothing ventured, nothing gained! In other words the potential for a goal exists, but unless it is manifested, unless it is actualized, unless the attempt is made to fulfill it, it remains purely potential. There is no incarnation of it!

The greatest problem that underdeveloped countries have today is their overwhelming shortage of manifested potential. No incarnation of public health, industrialization, literacy, sanitation, scientific agriculture or social service. Think of some of the different countries of the world for a moment-----China, India, Brazil, the Congo, Nigeria----all abundantly wealthy countries in terms of natural resources, land and people, and yet they are still some of the most underdeveloped peoples of the world! The difference between them and ourselves is the difference of manifestation or incarnation. We are the incarnation of the highly industrialized modern technological nation with obviously manifested potential and they are not. We have incarnated our potential in millions of ways and they have not.

It's nothing to make fun of this underdevelopment or lack of actualized potential. Many has been the time in winter when we have stood rather helplessly looking at our automobile that wouldn't start, with neither the tolls nor the knowledge for that matter of how to get it to start. We must have called for "technical assistance" six or eight different times! Just think what it would be like if something happened to the power plant that supplies our electricity, or to the water mains that supply our water as it did for some of us two weeks ago, or to the gas mains that supply our gas for heat and cooking. We might still have the potential for utilizing electricity, water and gas in our homes, but that's as far as it would go.It would just be potential and nothing more!

Incarnation then, means first of all the manifestation of potential. Secondly, it means the embodiment of a concept or quality.

In "Ministers of Mercy", by Fern Babcock Grant, a nation's most balanced resource is its children and youth. Its future depends upon their vitality, training and vision.

We couldn't ask for a more comprehensive statement than that for a view of what our nation is to become. Each child, as each nation, harbors a tremendous potential within itself that must become manifested if its future is to become better than its past.

This is simply another way of saying that we have to make our concepts concrete, if we are to understand them. An abstraction has to become visible if we are to communicate what we mean or think. We can talk about courage all we want, or the need of it, but show us a woman who goes ahead working and raising her children after the death of her husband, or a man who knows he's dying of cancer yet who goes on working as long as he can and making provision for his family after his death and we will understand what courage is. When we wish to communicate most effectively with another person we have to incarnate or embody the idea in such a way that a form becomes demonstrated to the thought of another and the most adequate way to do this is to register the effect upon the senses of a person.

Do you recall the method Jesus used to embody a particular concept or quality? He used parables for this purpose. When he wanted to talk with people about the concept of greed, for example, and its self-destroying quality, he talked about a rich man who kept building bigger and bigger barns in which to store his surplus crops. When he wanted to talk about the concept of pride and the insidiousness of its poison upon the lives of righteous men, he talked about a pharisee who went to the temple to pray and who thought he was praying when he was only reciting his own virtues while the man who was really praying was one who stood in utter humility and confessed to the wrongs he had committed. When he wanted to talk about hypocrisy and the evil effects of saying one thing and doing another he had only to lower his eyes in incredulous disbelief at what the righteous men of his faith were demanding and to suggest instead that the one among them who had never been guilty of sin cast the first stone. When he wanted to talk about the concept of concern for those who needed help he retold what his disciples had done for others of visiting the sick, the shut-ins, the lonely, giving food and drink to those who had nothing. He told of a man who has lost one of this sheep and had left all of the others alone while he searched for the one that was lost until he found it. When he wanted to talk about the concept of forgiving love and the quality of understanding that is like unto God himself, he told of a son who had taken all of his inheritance and spent everything he had----all of his hard-earned money of his father in one bodily excess after another and yet when he returned home his father was overjoyed to see him and welcomed him with open arms back into his household! Whenever Jesus spoke he attempted to give his abstract concepts embodiment and meaning for his hearers so that they could understand and the truth became self-evident.

The final meaning that I would suggest incarnation has is that we may see God in human form. A story is told of a little girl who was being put to bed one night and she was afraid of the dark. "Don't be afraid of the dark, said her mother. "God is with you." "I know," said the little girl, "but I want some one with a face." This is the desire quite typical of most persons. When God is spoken of it was with a face; with characteristics we can see, with traits we can follow, with an example ever before us.

If you were asked to describe an ideal, what would you reply? How would you characterize your religious ideals? When the author of John's Gospel grappled with this problem he came up with this idea "the word became flesh and dwelt among us." This was an ancient Hellenistic view of the union between flesh and spirit. The Greeks had looked out upon the world and had seen how the obvious was only a sign of the hidden, the spirit of God at work in the world. And for the Greeks, the highest illustration of what life could be like would have to be seen in as close a unity between the ideal and the real world as possible.

As the disciples thought back upon the life of Jesus they recalled what he had said, what he had done, and what kind of a man he was. They saw his will had become as completely subjected to the will of God as possible. They saw his quest for truth and the meaning of human action in the light of God's purpose as synonymous. They looked at Jesus and saw the spirit of God at work in the life of their great friend and teacher so that they thought if ever God were to take human form he would be exactly like Jesus. And thus when they looked at him they thought they saw God in human form.

Sir Edward Burne-Jones, a great artist of the British Empire during the nineteenth century wrote artists paint our God for the world. There's a lump of greasy pigment at the end of Michelangelo's hog-bristle brush and by the time it has been laid on the stucco, there was something that all men with eyes could recognize as Devine. It was the power of bringing God into the world giving God incarnation!

"Old Words With New Meaning: Sin"

"In holy books we read how God hath spoken to holy men in many different ways. But hath the present world no sign or token? Is God quite silent in these latter days?"

God is not silent, we have simply not been able to understand him with the words we've heard and used. We cannot understand because the meaning of the words of our religious vocabulary have become obtuse and obscure, unintelligible to us in today's world. We are still using terms that do not have eternal significance simply through their use, but unless they are up-dated, unless their meaning is made consistent with our understanding today, they are worse than empty; they are irrelevant.

Since we're on the subject, I might just as well confess my own uneasiness about the religious vocabulary that we still have. It's the vocabulary of an ancient aristocracy. Lord, kingdom, master, servant, terms that impart a particular view of life and which have certain connotations that simply do not fit modern times. We have neither kings nor nobles; we have neither slaves nor servants. We have neither a kingdom nor a holy city! And yet these words are those we're expected to utter. I'm sorry, but I can't! Whenever we read about persons trying to justify their resistance to social change upon some biblical text, is it any wonder? They're basing it upon a certain concept of life which is no longer at all alien to the same position that they are maintaining.

There's a very interesting book that's come out several years ago entitled, "What the Butler Saw," by E. S. Turner. It's a catalogue of life in the 18th century England where the division between the aristocracy and the lower classes was as pronounced as any in human history. In the servants' quarters this favorite New Testament text of the aristocracy was hung "to convince the lower classes that drudgery was part of the divine order and should be performed with diligence and thanks." The text was Ephesians 6: 5-6. "Servants be obedient to them that are your masters according to the flesh, with fear and trembling, in singleness of your heart, as unto Christ. Not with eye service, as men pleasers, but as the servants of Christ, doing the will of God from the heart."

I can't help but remember what Dr. Howard Thurman, Dean of the Boston University Chapel told us once. He was raised by his grandmother and she had some very definite ideas about what young Howard should and should not read. One author he could not read was the Apostle Paul. His grandmother knew her Bible and she knew what Paul had said about slaves and servants being content with their lot. She didn't want her grandson to grow up believing he was to be content, satisfied with his lot. She knew the history of her people too well and her own experience working for white people because she and her grandson, Dr. Howard Thurman were Negroes!

The continuing tragedy of human history comes in part from the continued usage of words that have lost their present meaning yet convert concepts that are outmoded, ancient relics like continually rattling skeletons that should have been long since buried!

Let us consider our third old word this morning to see what new meaning may be derived from it. The word is sin. It's thrown around so loosely that its meaning becomes blurred and obscure. It has long been associated with Adam in the old saw, "In Adam's Fall, we sinned all!" As if sin were an inheritable characteristic! This explains nothing and confuses the realistic issue of sin, by blaming it upon Adam for any sin we might commit and thereby absolving ourselves from any responsibility for our actions. This is not only too easy a solution to the problem of sin, it's also not true.

One of the first meanings we find sin has is that of behavior contrary to accepted ideals. In the book of James we find this meaning of sin spelled out. "Whoever knows what is right to do and fails to do it, for him it is sin." There is in this meaning then, the necessity of making a choice between two alternatives. Do you realize the necessity of choice that's involved in being moral? Most of us have never really tried to see whether or not we are moral. Ours is the morality of an untried choice. We've not been faced with the choice to sin or not to sin. We've not been offered the conflict that comes from considering a type of behavior contrary to accepted ideals.

In John Milton's Paradise Lost, Adam and Eve are discussing with one another the limits of privileged living on their island of Paradise. Adam is attempting to expel the wisdom of God in restricting their knowledge in order to remain at peace and in harmony within this paradise. But Eve replies, "And what is Faith, Love, Virtue unassisted? And what is Faith, Love, Virtue if they remain untried?

This is one of the risks we run if we are truly free to make a decision about whether our choice is consistent with our ideals, or contrary to them.

We're all familiar with the man who went overseas and behaved contrary to many of his accepted ideals because he confused license for freedom. He faced a choice and without the pressures of environment around him to keep him loyal to his ideals, he acted contrary to them. Going native is simply a euphemism for saying he's adopted behavior contrary to his ideals.

We're all familiar with the man who goes overseas and behaves contrary to many of his accepted ideals because he confuses license for freedom. He's faced with a choice and without the pressures of environment around him to keep him loyal to his ideals, he acts contrary to them. Going native is simply a euphemism for saying he's adopted behavior contrary to his ideals.

At one of our MYF meetings years ago, Dick Phillips told us that dating standards were periodically a matter of decision; of choice. What are our limits going to be? If we understand how our emotions respond to physical stimulation in a step by step process of steady increase we can use our minds to decide what our limits should be. Because we know once we're on the sex escalator it's practically impossible to get off. The problems arise when we act contrary to our accepted ideals. If you accept the ideal of sobriety and yet let yourself be influenced to go off on a bender; if you admire good health and the feeling of well-being that comes from sound habits of eating and exercise and you pick up the habit of smoking, going without sleep and staying up until all hours of the night; if you anticipate a self-fulfilling marriage where faith and love for each other is founded upon an abiding trust and confidence in one another and you allow yourself to be used by a man who seems interested or indulges with any woman who will, then you've made each of your ideals an impossibility that you'll never be able to reach. And you'll literally be in a state of sin.

The second meaning that sin has is the failure to fulfill our potential. This has already been implied in what has just been said. Whenever we have any ideals that was not fulfilled then they are simply potential. And so long as they are only potential then we are in a state of sin. If Saul had remained Saul and had not become Paul, then he would have continued to be in a state of sin. If Mary Magdalene had remained a prostitute she would not have fulfilled her potential of becoming a saint. If Peter had returned to his fishing after Jesus' death then the potential of his faith and ours might not have been revealed.

If each great saint of the church had not been what he was, it is doubtful we would be here today. I've never gotten over the statement made by a psychology professor some years ago when he said "A person has far more mental capacity than he ever puts to use. We are only a fraction of the potential ability we have either because of our environment or because of psychological reasons which inhibit broader uses of our mental abilities." Whenever I find myself growing contented and satisfied with a few minor accomplishments, I always think of his words and realize there is yet a long way to go....

Some years ago a woman, who was in a state of feeling sorry for herself, told me she just couldn't understand why God allowed her husband to die. He was such a good man. He had no bad habits. He never cursed or smoked or argued. He had no enemies. He was a good man. Why did he have to die, she kept asking? I miss him so much. Of course she missed him. You can't help but grow attached to each other when you live together for more than fifty years! As we talked about her husband and what they had done together all of these years, I couldn't help but feel doubly sorry for her. They had always done things together. "If he didn't want to go somewhere, they wouldn't go. If he wanted to paint the house, they painted the house. Life was just perfect together," she said. But now she was alone. Without her husband for the first time. They had no children so that she had no immediate family to turn to, to help fill the void; the utter lonely emptiness seemed more than she could bear. It's easy to say they were too close to each other. They depended too much upon each other. They lived in splendid isolation together too long. But this is exactly what had happened so that now she was desperately reaching out not for some meaning to life that is no longer there; reaching for love, companionship and the potential warmth of other human relationships that have been too long neglected.

We find this unfulfilled potential among ministers as well. There are those who are too easily contented; too quickly satisfied with the comforts of a friendly congregation to say anything that might offend anyone or to point out any problem areas within a neighborhood or community. They never do bring forth the potential of their faith because they wish to avoid controversy.

It was Dr. William Barclay who wrote about the meaning of sin as unfulfilled potential. "To fail to do one's best as workman; to fail to be as good a father, mother, son, daughter as one might have been; to fail to use and to develop the gifts of hand and eye, mind and brain that God has given us, in any way to fall short of the best that we could be is a sin."

The final meaning that sin has is that of the suppression of truth. It's one of those psychological peculiarities that we find when a person participates in a conscious deviation from morality, he unconsciously attempts to compensate for what he himself has done wrong by suppressing other instances of wrong-doing in other people. In other words, a person tries to suppress the truth about himself/herself by taking out his or her guilt on someone else. The Capo of the Nazi concentration camps were the guards who were the most ruthless because in their ill-treatment of the inmates for the least infraction of any rule or for attempting to steal bread, they could suppress the truth about themselves by saying, "See, you have to treat them cruelly otherwise they get out of hand!"

"The Ashes of Suffering"

Dr. Ralph Sockman once wrote of the time several years ago when he was visiting in an upstate city in New York State, on a bitterly cold winter night it was ten below zero and the roads were icy. His host's son and his fiancee had driven over from Cornell some thirty miles away. Before they started back, his host went down to the furnace room and brought a bucket of aches to put in their car so that if they got stuck on the slippery road, the ashes would give the tires some grip. Dr. Sockman then went on to write, "Similarly the ashes of suffering have to be carried on the journey of life so that faith, hope and love can keep going."

You have to carry them with you to give you traction when you again get stuck in a new area of suffering. People try to escape from suffering. They think they can avoid the necessity of it, flee from the reality of it. In Aldous Huxley's book "Brave New World" he pictured a world where all harsh and painful features of life have been removed. the Controller says to a recalcitrant man called Savage about this new world. "It's Christianity without tears." Savage replies, "But tears are necessary. You got rid of them. You just abolish the slings and arrows. It's too easy. I don't want comfort. I want God. I want poetry. I want real danger.

I want freedom. I want goodness. The controller replied, "You're claiming the right to be unhappy. " Savage retorted, "All right then, I'm claiming the right to be unhappy!"

Imagine what kind of a world it would be without hardships! Without pain our bodies would have no warning system. Without danger there would be no adventure in an undertaking. Without friction our cars would not start. Without tears our eyes could not see nor would they shine.

Suffering is a very vital and necessary part of life. This is not to say, however, that all that happens of evil and hardship to which we are heir is to be viewed as a discipline of us or as a means of bringing forth some purpose of God. So often we find persons who are smug enough to state that someone else's hardship is a means God has to teach that person a certain kind of lesson. How can you say that when a little child is stricken with polio, or an airplane crashes killing all on board, this is an act of God? How can you say that the earthquake which takes thousands of lives in various countries around the world each year was an act of God? And yet we hear these things said over and over again. Whenever anything goes wrong very seriously, or we've reached the point where we can find no other explanation, then we say, oh well, that was an act of God! We lay the blame on him and absolve ourselves from all responsibility. But before we consider a few of the values of suffering let us differentiate between the types of evil we find human beings experience. There is first, the type called moral evil. Where, due to various choices that individuals have made, some evil, some suffering results. A person who imperils the necessities of his/her family so that he/she can have those few extra beers night after night can easily be seen where he/she contributes to the evil of neglect we all deplore! There is a direct relationship between this person's choices and the results. Or if a person is speeding down the highway and is suddenly confronted with another car stalled on the road ahead and is unable to stop but slams into the other car killing the occupants. We can see where the speed, the act of haste has caused disaster even while disaster was not intended. The suffering was caused by a willful act. Or a boy gets into trouble because his father cared nothing for him. He wouldn't show any concern for his son. He didn't care if he got into trouble. Oh he threatened his son often enough with dire consequences, but he never acted as if he really loved his son. He just let him do what he [pleased. He never so much as deprived him of any of his privileges. It's little wonder that the son must suffer from the strictures of the law when his father did not begin to teach him the limits of privilege he would eventually have to learn for himself as an adult. The first type of suffering results as choice and may be called moral evil, where people determine the evil which results from their day by day choices.

The second type of evil may be called natural evil, or the type over which no individual human being has any control. This would be due to storms, floods, earthquakes, tidal waves, and certain types of disease, etc. or any evil that has no human will at the root of it. Whenever this natural evil occurs we are speechless, unable to grasp its meaning nor can we understand its purpose. Between these two types of evil all kinds of suffering can be divided that you and I or anyone else will ever experience.

Consider now some of the values that can come from suffering. First, suffering can make us humble. Suffering makes it possible for us to learn what another person experiences, what another person goes through. The poet

Oliver Wendell Holmes once said he was one who did not take naturally to religion. He felt he had no propensity for religion just as certain persons have no ear for music. But he was turned toward religion "By the discipline of trials in the life of outward circumstance," he had to endure. "It was needful that I should learn the meaning of the text, 'When the Lord liveth he chasteneth.'" The force of circumstance can subdue our pride as nothing else can.

Consider for a moment what happens when a person has an uncontrollable temper. Think of all of the harm he can do in one of his explosions! The feelings that can hurt; the joyous attitudes that can be shattered; the affection that can be ruptured; the lives that can be destroyed from an outburst of uncontrollable anger!

Do you remember the story of Moses? How he grew up in the court of Pharaoh and one day upon an impulse of anger slew an Egyptian who was mistreating an Israelite and hastily buried him in the sand? The next day as Moses was walking along the road he saw two of his Hebrew countrymen in a quarrel. When he criticized "the man that did the wrong" he cried, "Do you mean to kill me as you killed the Egyptian?" Moses than knew that his evil deed of temper had been discovered. He also felt that his own fellow Hebrews were not grateful for what he had sone for them. Hence, in dejection and bitterness Moses left Egypt and became a sheep herder in Midian.

It was while dwelling in the exile of his own bitterness of spirit that his people did not understand him that Moses has an experience of God. It seemed to him that he felt God wished him to return to Egypt to help his people. From dwelling upon his own pride and self-pity, Moses' spirit became uplifted. He who had withdrawn from those who needed him went back to become their leader in a great exodus from Egypt. The hot temper which had gotten him into trouble as a young man became so disciplined that he led his countrymen for forty years through countless irritations on that grueling track across the wilderness toward Canaan. The secret of his patient and preserving leadership was "He endured as seeing him who is invisible." (Heb.11:27) The private suffering of spirit which Moses had borne gave him the humility necessary to become a great leader of his people!

Dr. Sockman raised an excellent question concerning the fact that suffering does not always make us humble but can make us bitter as well, when he asked, "When painful misfortune comes, does it humble us or merely humiliate us? If it humbles us, we can find the value in experience. If it humiliate us, we push ourselves further into the morass of suffering through self-pity.

The second value that we find in suffering is that it forces us to outgrown our complacency. Take a look at a child for a moment. Suppose a baby had no interest in moving about; in crawling on the floor; in drawing himself/herself up and standing on his/her wobbly legs. Suppose a child were perfectly satisfied with continually sitting on the floor or staying exactly where you put him or her and content hour by hour with the simple amusements of his/her toys. Suppose the child never wondered about what that intriguing color was on the table. Suppose he/she never tried raising himself/herself up and climbing out of his/her crib. Would you be satisfied with a completely complacent, inert child? Would you be pleased with the fact that your child never tried to walk? Would you feel safe, comfortable, secure in knowing that nothing would happen to your child at all? O course not! But there are plenty of parents who seem to think this is exactly how they want their children to be. No risks, no fears, no problems, no troubles, no difficulties, no hardships of any kind! But I ask you, how can a child learn to walk, except by suffering a few falls or even many falls for that matter? One grandparent I've heard say "If there is any absolutely painless way of rearing children, grandparents would surely have discovered it!"

Suffering forces us out of our complacency. We cannot stand still. We cannot control all of the possible dangers we face in life. We cannot rest securer, comfortable and safe in our own little worlds, without destroying the very things we cherish most!

Many years ago I called in a home where the parents had just told me their youngest son had not done well in school. The father said "He just won't study. There's too much television and too little study. If a favorite program comes on then off he goes to watch it. He just doesn't spend any time with his lessons!"

I couldn't help but wonder why the boy was doing poorly in school. Where were the parental voices, the authority that said, "Work comes before play? After you've done your homework you can watch T.V." I could almost see what a supervisor of Public School Teachers meant when he said a couple of years earlier, the worst thing that can happen to our world would be for our children to grow up to be like us!" I saw happening in the life of the son, what had happened in the life of the father years before. He had not been confronted with the need to outgrow his complacency and spend any time with his studies either!

It hurts to grown and sometimes it means that we grow beyond what we originally expected or what others expected. Ask any father or mother how it feels to see their son or daughter leave the home and set up on of their own. I've seen these problems in home after home. There is a loneliness that nothing can fulfill. There's a gap nothing can ever replace when that boy or girl outgrows the surroundings in which you might have felt he or she was always a part!

The final value than can come from suffering is that we become aware of our dependence upon God. Dr. Peter Bertocci, a professor at Boston University, in his book, "Philosophy of Religion" wrote of religion that "It is the father that God is the ultimate Personal Creator and Sustainer of all values. Religion is never an escape from suffering and hardship, but it is a fellowship in joy and suffering for ends approved by God." Nothing could be more true of the fellowship in joy and suffering which has brought the reality of man's dependence upon God more completely than the work of men like Gordon Seagrave. He was born in Burma from a long line of missionaries going back three generations. After completing his studies in the United States he returned to Burma using a basketful of instruments that had been thrown out of the operating room at Johns Hopkins Medical School. The operating superintendent decided to clean out all of the useless broken-down surgical instruments that could no longer be repaired. Dr. Seagrave, remembering Burma and the instruments that were now extinct there, asked if he might have the basketful and his request was granted and for the next five years these cast off instruments were used to do all of the surgical work he had to do in the primitive hospital on the Chinese border. Dr. Seagrave was not interested in the fanfare of what he was doing. He simply recognized what needed to be done and he did it! The hospital he and his wife inherited when they first went to Burma was a rotting wooden building with twenty bare, wooden beds. The best they could say was that "If Namkham wasn't what we wanted it to be, we would get off to an early start and do something about it. And do something about it, he did. He had served in Burma almost forty years through plagues, epidemics, warfare, poverty, ignorance and as many kinds of diseases imaginable to bring help to the people for whom there had been no help. But of all that Dr. Seagrave had done for the people of northern Burma, nothing surpassed the training of Burmese girls as nurses so that during World War II with their great skill and courage, they won the hearts of all who saw them work. These former ignorant, unwashed and by the traditional scale of importance, "Lower than male dogs" girls, "surrounded by their racial and creedal differences for the good of their country, and showed a spirit of selfless, untiring and loving service to the sick and wounded of all races.

Suffering makes us aware that our ultimate dependence is upon God. Dr. Paul Tillick, in his book "Shaking the Foundations" wrote, "the depth of suffering is the door to the depth of truth! Pain can be a teacher and a purifier. God brings men into deep waters, not to drown them, but to cleanse them."

Katherine Mansfield wrote at the end of her long and fatal illness, "What must one do so that suffering can be overcome? One must submit. Take it. Be overwhelmed. Accept it full. Make it part of life. Everything that we really accept undergoes a change. So suffering must become love….. must put my agony into something that can change it."

Take the ashes of your suffering with you. You may need them again…..

Old Words With New Meaning: Incarnation

"In holy books we read how God hath spoken
To Holy men in many different ways;
But hath the present world no sign or token?
Is God quite silent in these latter days?"

We shall consider again how God is still speaking in these latter days. The question was raised following a service of who decides which words have lost their meaning? It's a legitimate question and shows that the person is giving very serious thought to the consequences of this series of sermons. Another question that might also be asked concerning this proposal to review our religious vocabulary is if various practices or words have lost their meaning is this any reason for dropping them? How can we drop some of these old hymns that are a part of our tradition?

These are good questions and they really come to the heart of the matter very quickly, but what you do with your religious practices, which words you accept and which ones you reject depends upon what your view of religion is.

If you are a fundamentalist, you can't tolerate even an iota of change. This would be heresy for you. If you are a traditionalist, you feel ancient sites and words must continue because they were part of the tradition of your fathers and. therefore, holy to you! To drop them would be a sacrilege.

If you are a naturalist in the theological sense, then you repeatedly test your faith in the light of new experience arising from related causal factors.

If you are a liberal, then you reserve the right to question any precept, examine any truth claim, evaluate every doctrine in the light of other ares of knowledge and experience and to review the tradition and vocabulary of religion periodically to allow the spirit of the age to speak anew to the heart of men and women.

There is no single word or series of words that can ever fully express truth at any one time, for truth is never total or complete, but unfolding and fragmentary at any point of time. And then, as new truth is discovered, it is incorporated into the collective body of knowledge with old truths, no longer true or acceptable, replaced with newer more complete expressions of truth in the present until some newer or even better expressions of it comes along.

Sir Isaac Newton expressed the epitome of humility in the fact of continuously unfolding truth when he said of himself and his own great scientific and anatomical discoveries, "I do not know what I may appear in the world; but to myself I seem to have been only like a boy playing on the seashore, and diverting myself in mow and then finding a smoother pebble or a prettier shell than ordinary, whilst the great ocean of truth lay all undiscovered before me."

Let us consider then, the finding of some smoother pebbles or prettier shells of meaning then ordinary from the second old word of our series that needs to have new meaning drawn out of it if its truth is to be seen today and if we are to hear God speak through it in these latter days. The second word we shall consider is incarnation. It's footage is in the old Christian doctrine that God became man in Jesus Christ. But so much confusion and difference of opinion exists among different authorities on this point that it's necessary for us to clarify its meaning.

The first meaning that incarnation has is that of the manifestation of potential/ I'm sure we've all heard the old cliche, "Nothing ventured, nothing gained." But have you ever considered how very true this is? Without trying, without making an effort, without spending ourselves in moving toward a particular goal, no goal is accomplished. Nothing ventured, nothing gained! In other words, the potential of a goal exists, but unless it is manifested, unless it is actualized, unless the attempt is made to fulfill it, it remains purely potential. There is no incarnation of it.

The greatest problem that underdeveloped countries have today is their overwhelming shortage of manifested potential. No incarnation of public health, industrialization, literacy, sanitation, scientific agriculture or social service. Think of some of the different countries of the world for a moment. India, the Congo, Brazil, Nigeria, all abundantly wealthy countries in terms of natural resources, land and people and yet they are still some of the most underdeveloped peoples in the world!

The difference between anthem and ourselves is the difference of manifestation or incarnation. We are the incarnation of the highly industrialized, modern technological nations with obviously manifested potential and they are not. We have incarnated our potential in millions of ways and they have not.

It's nothing to make fun of this underdevelopment or lack of actualized potential. Many has been the time this winter when I stood rather helplessly by looking at our automobile that wouldn't start, with neither the tools nor the knowledge for that matter, of how to get it to start. We must have called for "technical assistance" six or eight different times! Just think what it would be life if something happened to the power plant that supplies our electricity, or to the water mains that supply our water as if did for some os us recently. Or to the gas mains that supply our gas for beast and cooking. We might still have the potential for utilizing electricity, water and gas in our homes, but that's as far as it would go. It would just be potential and nothing more!

Incarnation then, means first and foremost the manifestation of potential.

Secondly, incarnation means the embodiment of a concept or quality. In "Ministries of Mercy" by Babcock Grant a nation's most valuable resource is its children and youth. Its future depends upon the vitality, training and vision of our youth. We could not ask for a more comprehensive statement than this for a view of what our nation is to become. Each child, as each nation, harbors a tremendous potential within itself that must become manifested if tis future is to become better than its past.

This is simply another way of saying that we have to make our concepts concrete, if we are to understand them. An abstraction has to become visible if we are to communicate what we mean or think. We can talk about courage all we want, or the need of it, but show us a woman who goes ahead working and raising her children after the death of her husband, or a man who knows he is dying of cancer yet goes on working as long as he can and making provision for his family after his death and we understand what courage is. When we wish to communicate most effectively with another we have to incarnate or embody the idea in such a way that a form becomes demonstrable to the thought of another and the most adequate way to do this is to register the effect upon the senses of a person.

Do you recall the method Jesus used to embody a particular concept or quality? He used parables for this purpose. When he wanted to talk with people about the concept of greed, for example, and its self-destroying quality he talked about a rich man who kept building bigger and bigger barns in which to store his surplus crops. When he wanted to talk about the concept of pride and the insidiousness of its poison upon the lives of righteous men, he talked about a pharisee who went to the temple to pray and who thought he was praying when he was simply reciting his own virtues while the man who was really praying was one who stood in utter humility and confession of the wrongs he had committed. When he wanted to talk about hypocrisy and the evil of effects of saying one thing and doing another he had only to lower his eyes in incredulous disbelief at what righteous men of his faith were demanding and to suggest instead that the one among them who had never been guilty of sin cast the first stone. When he wanted to talk about the concept if concern for those who needed help he retold what his disciples had done for others of visiting the sick, the shut-ins, the lonely; giving food and drink to those who had nothing. He told them of a man who had lost one of this sheep and had left all of the others alone while he searched for the one that was lost until he found it. When he wanted to talk about the concept of forgiving love and the quality of understanding that is like unto God himself, he told of a son who had taken all of his inheritance and spent everything he had----all of the hard-earned money of his father----in one bodily excess after another and yet when he returned home his father was overjoyed to see him and welcomed him with open arms aback into his household! Whenever Jesus spoke he attempted to give his abstract concepts embodiment and the meaning for his hearers was understood or became self-evident.

The final meaning that incarnation has is that we see God in human form. A story is told of a little girl who was being put to bed one night and she was afraid of the dark. "Don;t be afraid," said her mother, "God is with you." "I know," said the little girl. "But I want some one with a face." This is a desire quite typical of most persons. When God is spoken of we want someone with a face; with characteristics we can see; with traits we can follow; with an example ever before us!

If you were asked to describe an ideal, what would you reply? How would you characterize your religious ideals? When the author of John's Gospel grappled with this problem he came up with the idea "The word became flesh and dwelt among us." This was an ancient Hellenisitic view of the union between flesh and spirit. The Greeks had looked out upon the world and had seen how the obvious was only a sign of the hidden, the spirit of God at work in the world. And for the Greeks, the highest illustration of what life could be like would have to be seen in as close a unity between the ideal and the real world as possible.

As the disciples thought back upon the life of Jesus, as they recalled what he had said, what he had done and what kind of a man he was, they saw his will had become as completely subjected to there well of God as possible. They saw his quest for truth and the meaning of human action in the light of God's purpose as synonymous with what they saw as they looked at Jesus and saw the spirit of God t work in the life of their great friend and teacher so that they thought if ever God were to take human form. he would be exactly like Jesus. And thus, when they looked at him, they thought they saw God in human form.

Sir Edward Burne-Jones that great artist of Great Britain during the 19th century one wrote the that artists point God for the world. There's a lump of greasy pigment at the end of Michelangelo's hog-bristle brush, and by the time it has been laid on the stucco, there is something that all men with eyes recognize as divine. It is the power of bringing God into the world giving him incarnation!

Is It A Blessed Confusion?

Halford Luccock, a preacher's professor at the Yale Divinity School once told a neighbor of his who had worked himself up to the belief that he was extremely sensitive to noise. He made more noise than anyone else on the block, complaining about the noise the neighbors made. But he never noticed the noise which he made! He had a highly selective attention capacity. He had three children and they made a lot of noise. Dr. Luccock discovered only gradually what the man really wanted above all was to restore the kingdom of quiet that had prevailed before the children joined the family parade! This couldn't be done. For family life, he said, is like universal history. It's divided into two epochs, B. C. and A. D. meaning "before children and after the deluge!"

A family with children is not a kingdom of peace. It is a democracy of noise; "A blessed confusion!" Family life…
..A blessed confusion!

There are families that I've observed where there seems to be plenty of confusion, but in no sense the thought that it may be blessed! In some families there is the constant refrain of "You can't do that because I said no!" In others, the raised hand symbolizing threat, attempted through the use of force irrespective of any other consideration. Then there is the family where one or both parents constantly say, "If we only didn't have kids to take care of, how nice life might be!"

And they say this continually within hearing of the children….."If only I didn't have to take care of…..I might be able to do some of these other things….." Is family life viewed as a blessed confusion for these people? I'm afraid not…..

On the occasion of the beginning of National Family Week, I should like to share with you some thoughts concerning family life. You are probably right in asking what do you know about family life? You've only recently had one!

I'll admit I feel like the bachelor who wrote the line, "Order is heaven's first law." Speaking on this subject, I've had some experience as a member of a family and we have had our own as well. As time has gone by I like to think we've experienced the hypothesis that a family is a blessed confusion!

The first thought that comes to mind on this subject is a family should be planned. This has been said before but should be said again and again. It's a mistake to think a family just comes about naturally. It does, of course, in one sense. The parents carry out the biological action and the children will follow. But to think we can do nothing about when they should come and how often, is a mistake. You and I (as a couple) decided the date of birth of our children. It doesn't just happen!

It reminds me of a conversation I had with a young mother who said, "The children just keep coming…..I've been to a doctor, but what he says doesn't seem to help. It was only after my third child in three years that I found out he was Catholic!"

As you well know, we need to plan for the arrival of our children and also for their futures! We have to be sure we are able to buy them food and clothing that they'll need. Will we be able to have a pleasant home for them? Will we be able to provide them with opportunities of growth in body and mind we are so necessary for the wholesome development of their personalities. If we do not undertake to consider these requirements we have to ask ourselves are we really preparing ourselves for the growth and development of our families? Can our families be part of those whom we can truly say are among the blessed on earth?

Secondly, are you sure of your role in the family? There is little so devastating to family life than the confusion which results from members of the family having lost the sense of knowing what their role is in the family. I have known couples who feel at a complete loss to know what they should do in their family life. They seem to have lost the knowledge or perhaps had never had it that they are the loving husband of their wives and and the fathers of their children. I know of one who has completely lost his knowledge of what his role is in the family. It's a pathetic state of affairs to be in. He doesn't know how to exercise any authority in his family. He's totally dependent upon his wife to make all of the decisions not only for the whole family, but him as well. He's abdicated his role as father and head of the household for a position of complete dependence upon his wife. His children taunt him and make fun of him. They're as confused as he is to find their father is like a child himself. He's not a man with confidence in himself. He cannot bring himself to use any discipline upon his children. He fears a loss of love for him if he tried to act as a father should. He seems to have forgotten only a man can be a father.

Take the role a woman plays in family life. Notice how many women are confused about what their role in a family should be. Many of them are betwixt and between. Should they work outside of the home and help be a provider, or should they stay at home and take care of the house and concern themselves with the needs of their children and husband? What should I do, is the question she asks continually? She no longer seems to know what her role is. She seems to have forgotten only a woman can be a mother.

Do you know what your role is in the family? If not, life will be a confusion rather than a blessing. Are you satisfied with what you are doing in your family situation?

The third concept we should keep in mind about our role in the family is have we reminded ourselves what the purpose of family life really is? A great theologian and sociologist has written, "The crisis of modern family life will not be met until men and women intend responsible marriage, adequately prepare for it, and carry it out in good faith. Christian marriage is a permanent partnership in moral development and the joyous sharing of love and companionship between the parents and with the children who are brought into the family."

There is no substitute for family life; there is no simpler nor at the same time more difficult experience than fulfilling the purpose of family life. There is one church whose view of family life is essentially procreative human reproduction as the chief purpose of men and women in marriage. It's almost like saying we don't care about the quality of life, we just want life. And it's true, isn't it? Many people don't stop to think what the purpose of family life may be, that it's just a matter of having a few kids, a comfortable home, a steady job and as few problems as possible through the course of a lifetime? But is this the real purpose of family life? Notice what each of these things is….having a few kids, a comfortable home, a steady job, few problems….Not one of these items has anything to do with the quality of life involved! Family life is almost viewed as if a man were asked what he wanted more than anything else in the world. He replied, "Financial security for the rest of my life!"

We're always on the edge of something. We don't seem to get into the center of what life is for. We don't seem to remember what the purpose of life is. We don't even stop to realize what originally brought us together as a husband and wife…..It's somehow forgotten, pushed aside as impractical and irrelevant to life and we look at the outside of things. The kind of house we have, the amount of income we'll have, the avoidance of all difficulties and involvements other than what interests us answer…..You'll say, that's a preacher for you…..Always talking about it…..Then you'll promptly forget it before you leave this morning! You won't even think of it again as you ignore the other people in church today…You'll not even begin to think of it as your young son asks you if you'll come out and play with him this afternoon; you'll deny it as you tell your daughter she can't go out with so and so because you don't want her going out with anyone of that nationality. You'll continue to deny it even as you've done since you got her to say yes so many years ago. You say it was silly sentimentalism that ever allowed you to believe that family life could be the best way to describe why you felt about him…..But it's still the only purpose for which life was created! You children won't just evolve into a knowledge of to…..No matter how many vitamins, doctors, gadgets, toys, progressive public schools you give them. It still can never compensate for what the full-time vocation of the marriage pertness requires. Not even the two income family can buy it…..The way in which we speak of the purpose of family life reminds me of the allegory Hugh Price Hughes wrote concerning "The City of Everywhere." It is the tale of a man who might have been me. I dreamed one time of journeying to this metropolis. I arrived early one morning. It was cold. There were snow flurries on the ground and as I stepped from the train to the platform, I noticed that the baggage man and the Red Cap were warmly attired in heavy coats and gloves, but, oddly enough, they wore no shoes. My initial impulse was to ask the reason for this odd practice, but repressing it I passed into the station and inquired the way to the hotel. My curiosity, however, was immediately enhanced by the discovery that no one in the station wore any shoes. Boarding the streetcar, I saw my fellow travelers were likewise barefoot. Upon reaching the hotel, I found the bellhops, the clerk and the habitués of the place were all without shoes.

"Unable to restrain myself any longer, I asked the ingratiating manager what this practice meant. "

"What practice?" he asked.

"Why?" I said, pointing to his bare feet. "Why don't you wear any shoes in this town?"

"Ah," he said. "That's just it, why don't we?"

"But what's the matter? Don't you believe in shoes?" I asked.

"Believe in shoes, my friend! I should say we do. That is the first article of our creed, shoes. They are indispensable to the well-being of humanity. Such chilblains, cuts, sores, suffering as shoes prevent! It's wonderful!"

"Well, then why don't you wear them?" I asked bewildered.

"Ah," he said. "That's just it. Why don't we?"

"Just then, as we turned down a side street, I saw through a cellar window a cobbler actually making a pair of shoes. Excusing myself from my friend, I burst into the little shop and asked the shoemaker how it happened that his shop was not overrun with customers? He answered, "Nobody wants my shoes. They talk about them."

"Give me what pairs you already have," I said eagerly and paid him thrice the amount he had modestly asked. Hurriedly, I returned to my friend and proffered them to him, saying "Here, my friend, take one of these pairs which will surely fit you. Take them. Put them on. They will save you untold suffering."

He looked embarrassed; in fact, he was well-nigh overcome with chagrin.

"Ah, thank you," he said politely. "But you don't understand. It just isn't being done. The front families, well, I ....."

"But why don't you wear them?" I asked dumbfounded.

"Ah," said he. smiling with an accustomed ingratiating touch of practical wisdom, "That's just it, Why don't we?"

And coming out of the "City of Everywhere" into the here and now, over and over that query has rung in my ears! "Why don't we? Why don't we? Why don't we?"

"Why call ye me, Lord, Lord and do not the things I command you?"

Why aren't we fulfilling the purpose of Family Life?

A Drop Of Honey?

In William Wolf's book, The Almost Chosen People, he had Abraham Lincoln saying that the true approach to winning a man to your cause is first to "Convince him that you are his sincere friend. Therein is a drop of honey that catches his heart, which, say what he will, is the great road to his reason, and which, once gained, you will find but little trouble in convincing his judgment of the justice of your cause."

Once the heart has been captured, you can do or say what you will and no offense will occur. If you doubt the truth of this, simply look around you and notice what is taken, accepted, or done because the heart has been captured!

I'm often amazed, yet pleased with the fact that once the capturing of the heart has taken place a wife or a husband will put up with almost any cause her husband or his wife may have! "Thy people are my people, and thy God is my God," to use the words of Ruth.

In 1852 at a meeting of the Methodists of England at Brinton, William Booth stood before the entire conference and declared the church was not concerning itself sufficiently with the outcasts, the poverty stricken, the lost of the streets and byways of England. After he had finished his indictment against the disinterest of the church for the needs and welfare of the down and out, he was asked to withdraw his criticism of the church. As he stood up to give his reply, the sharp clear encouragement rang out from the balcony as his wife stood and shouted to him, "William, stand fast for I am with thee!" And William and Catherine Booth walked out of the Methodist Church to found the Salvation Army! Capture the heart and nothing can stand in your way if your cause is just.

Once the heart has been captured through friendship then the confrontation of issues may take place which could not be done before this foundation has been laid. In other words, in our relations with other people the cultivation of friendship should be first and only then can disputes be handled amicably. One of the cautions, probably, that each of our professors in seminary told us was that we were to get to know our people first and they were to know us before any controversial issues were to be preached. A year after my wife and I had accepted our appointment to our church, I went with a friend to visit a church that was considering him as its minister. My friend was a very out-spoken person. He was apt to tell you exactly what he thought on almost any subject whether he was talking about your intelligence or the place where you were living. He always said he was only interested in being absolutely honest, no matter how much it may hurt. Well, when he met with the various church officials and the pastoral relations committee he told them exactly where he stood theologically, socially, and economically point by point. There weren't many questions asked by any of the church officials since he had left neither doubt nor room for negotiation on any point. Following the meeting, the District Superintendent asked for a vote on how many of the officials would like to have him for their minister. You probably already know the outcome. Not a single person spoke out in his favor!

People do not want to be argued with or forced into changing their ways of living or points of view until they know you and you know them. And yet, instead of using a drop of honey, they insist on using a bucket of vinegar in their relationships with other people whom they do not know and who do not know them. How can we get along with others? What are some of the drops of honey which can be used to cultivate friendship, love, and persuasion? What can each one do to gain the great high road to another person's reason?

The first drop of honey which may be used is developing a genuine interest in people. Notice I said, "a genuine interest." This doesn't mean a phony interest simply made up for the moment and then cast off as soon as that person has left. We see plenty of this forced interest on occasion. A large social gathering is undoubtedly the place where more of this forced, transient interest is encountered than anywhere else! But the idea of a genuine interest in people means we become as interested in them as we are in ourselves.

Teddy Roosevelt was a man with very definite opinions about what he had to do as President, and yet he was recognized as an extremely able and affable man who could generate an immediate and genuine interest in another person. One of his colleagues told him that he and President McKinley were very much alike in that they never talked more than five minutes with any man without making him feel he was very much liked. To this Teddy Roosevelt replied, "I've never stopped to think about it, but I do believe I've never talked with a person for five minutes without liking him very much." He had a very sincere and genuine interest in people and was able to communicate this interest to others.

By taking a genuine interest in others we lift them toward heights they may never have known existed. Look at the interest Jesus had for people. Some of them were the most unpromising and unlikely people to win a popularity contest that you can imagine. And yet these were the very people whom we so highly prize today! Dr. Hugh Black. a great preacher from Union Seminary years ago said, "Jesus took men on their strongest side. He accepted the highest in them as representative of their true self. In the company of sinners, he dreamed of saints!"

When Benjamin Franklin was still a young man he was elected clerk of the Pennsylvania Assembly. Another member of influence and wealth made a speech against him and completely ignored him in the Assembly. In Franklin's autobiography he told how he handled this provocative conduct through active good will towards this person. Having heard that he had in his library a certain very scarce and curious book, I wrote him a note, expressing my desire of perusing that book and requesting that he would do me the favor of lending it to me for a few days. He sent it immediately. I returned it to him in a week with another note, expressing strongly my sense of the favor. When we next met in the Assembly, he spoke to me with great civility and he ever afterward manifested a readiness to serve me on all occasions, so that we became great friends and our friendship continued to his death.

Taking a genuine interest in people such as the interest shown us by our parents, teachers, and friends is the kind that can literally transform the world.

The second drop of honey that we can use is to put ourselves in the other person's position. Several years ago in Singapore, there were riots and civil strife of the worst sort as Chinese extremists fought pitched battles with British and Malay police in an effort to gain the independence of the island from the Federation of Malaya. Literally ten of thousands of people swarmed through the city for several days chanting anti-British slogans and demanding immediate independence. The leaders of the Chinese Community of Singapore (which was literally a Chinese city), refused to negotiate with the British administration or have any part in the Singapore government. The British Governor-General dissolved the City Council (predominantly European) and declared a general election to follow within a month. The resulting votes were predominantly in favor of the representatives and leaders of the Chinese People's Party…..the ones who had remained aloof from the previous administration. This election put these former extremists into positions of power held by the former British Administration. Most Europeans feared the worst would follow. But, strange as it may seem, the very fact of putting these extremists into the positions of responsibility for government in Singapore had an amazingly conservative effect upon them. Singapore today has a very smooth and well run administration working very closely with the authorities of the Malayan Federation. By literally being in the former administration's position, these Chinese party leaders discovered an appreciation for the responsibility of government that hey had been unable to understand previously. This was in the period prior to the independence of Malaysia and Singapore as independent nation-states.

Put yourself in another's place and you can't help but feel more sympathetic. Dr. Homer Miller in his book "Take a Look at Yourself" wrote "Among your friends are people who are unduly sensitive, people who make constant bids for sympathy, people who are carrying secret burdens which have colored their personalities, people who are arrested in their mental development and infantile in their emotional reactions, people who have been pampered by an anxious but well-meaning parent, people to whom, success has come too easily, people upon whom defeat and failure have fallen, people who are spiritually sick but do not know it, people who hide their candle under a bushel." The a ability to put ourselves in varying positions will spell the difference between sympathy or misunderstanding of other people. Think of it! The difference between understanding and misunderstanding can be discovered by each one of us as we put ourselves in another person's position.

Some years ago a young woman remarked a few short months after the tragic death of her husband. She was roundly criticized by everyone including her family who would not have anything to do with her for almost two years. They felt she had betrayed her love for her husband by, marrying so soon after his death. They simply couldn't understand how she could do such a thing. Little did they realize how hard it had been for her to face the future alone with two small children to raise, her husband's affairs to look after, and her own desperate need for someone to fill the void that had been so recently created within her life. Her own family's inability to help her in her greatest hours of need precipitated the step she took. By putting yourself in another's position you can at least understand him or her and why he or she does what they do. You may not always agree with what they do, but you will understand enough to understand why.

Some of you have heard this illustration before, but it's worth repeating. A great Iroquois Indian philosopher by the name of Red Cloud, speaking to an Assembly of Chiefs debating whether there should be war or peace with another nation counseled, "Until you have walked in the moccasins of another person you do not really know him or why he is doing what he does."

The final drop of honey that we can use is the exercise of continual good will. This is not easy to do. It means exhibiting good will even in the face of criticism or active hostility. By exercising continued good will,, even an enemy may be turned into a friend. Near the close of the Civil War some wounded soldiers of the Confederacy were prisoners at City Point. They discussed among themselves very bitterly the man whom they believed had caused the war. Not long after, President Lincoln came to visit City Point. He visited the soldiers of the Northern Army and did not forget the Rebel soldiers being cared for in the ward nearby. After he left, one of the southern soldiers sat up in bed and said" "Is that the kind of man we've been fighting against for four years? Why he even recognized us Rebels and treated us as well as any of his own." And yet, for Abraham Lincoln the exercise of continued good will even in the face of strong criticism was ever an active part of his entire life. He knew that the best way to get rid of an enemy is to make him a friend. As his good will became increasingly evident towards the South even when victory for the North became certain, he was severely taken to task by an elderly lady who rebuked him for speaking kind words for the South. "Why do you speak well of your enemies?" she demanded, Rather than destroy them?" To which Lincoln replied, "Why Madam, Do I not destroy my enemies when I make them my friends?"

A genuine interest in people, putting ourselves in another person's position, exercising good will in the face of criticism.....these are the drops of honey that catch the hearts and are the great high roads to reason!

What Is The Purpose
Of Government?

First of all, let us review not only what government does, but how it is structured in the United States. There are three levels of government: national (which has supreme authority over all other levels of government). The second level is that of the state governments which has its primary authority over the residents living within their borders. The third level and the one with which all persons have most contact is the local governing authorities: mayors, councils, and townships which supervise all activities of the local population under their jurisdiction. These activities include local police, firemen, assessors and jurisdiction over water, sewage, garbage disposal and the use of land in behalf of the local population.

Second, each of these entities has its prescribed authority, under law, to provide for the local general welfare of each locality. While a state government may take up the challenge of the authority exercised by the national government on a given issue, ultimately the final judgment rests with the federal authorities which supersede all lower levels of governance.

Third, each of these governing entities has the authority to impose upon the general public the laws and ordinances which these officials believe serve the best interests of the wider community over which they have authority. Each level of government may be challenged in the sequence of courts prescribed for each of these governing bodies by citizens who believe their rights have been violated. However, the ultimate legal authority rests with the United States Supreme Court. Should this court decide not to take a case submitted to it for consideration, then the judgment of the previous highest court prevails and must be accepted.

Fourth. the federal government is composed of three branches. The Congress (the House of Representatives and Senate) provides the ultimate authority in passing the laws governing all aspects of law set forth in their determination that such laws should apply to all persons living in the United States. These determinations are made by a majority vote of the members of the House of Representatives. The Senate, due to the difficulty of gaining the required majority vote to approve or disapprove of a law, has decided that the vote of sixty members alone can decide the vote in favor of or in apposition to the given law under consideration. The evolution of this system was started in the Constitution in which the framers decided that the initiation of any tax bills must be taken up first by the members of the House of Representatives since they were viewed as "closest" to the public which had elected them (the Congressional districts are much smaller than those of the Senate whose districts entail an entire state for each Senator) assuring that a greater number of Representatives were to consider this legislation, 435 members of Congress verses 100 Senators) first. The belief was that

Representatives were much closer to their constituents than were Senators, therefore they were more likely to consider taxes more carefully than the members of the Senate. The Senate takes up legislation only after it has been passed by the House of Representatives. Because of the opposition of a minority of Senators, they can delay or even prevent such passage. The Senate has adopted the sixty member rule to shut off a filibuster. There have to be sixty members in favor of shutting down further debate on a given bill (a Senator or a group of Senators would otherwise continue to speak without let up). It is only possible for a bill to become law if it has been passed by both the House and Senate.

The Federal government is headed by a President elected by American citizens aged eighteen or older. He/she is both the head of government and the head of state (the first is the initiator and leader of his/her party. The latter is to perform and host ceremonial functions). The Office of the President has taken on an enormously powerful role in modern times. Not only does his/her administration undertake to write legislation or propose bills which he/she thinks are important for the country, but he/she works with the Congress to undertake laws which he/she believes will aid in improving the lives of his/her fellow Americans or the status of the United States around the world. With the advance of modern telecommunications, transportation, and modern weaponry the position of the United States in the world has taken on an inordinate amount of importance given the size, power and influence which this country has had over the rest of the world since the end of World War II. The success of the President as a candidate for election places him/her in a unique position of reflecting what the electorate wishes to accomplish in the four year term to which he/she has been elected. Given the election campaign, he/she reflects the promise of what he/she would prefer to do if he/she should be successful in winning the required number of states to be approved by the electoral college for his/her term in office for four years.

The Supreme Court is the last of the three branches into which the United States Government is divided as separate but equal to the other two branches. It was assumed originally that this branch of the government would settle disputes arising between the other branches, the States, and lastly, among the citizens of the country in contention with each other. Hence, the appointment of the Court's members was for life rather than being elected for a specific term of office. The fear was the members of the Court would be too wary of antagonizing potential voters if they had to seek reelection after a given term in office. This has resulted in establishing the Supreme Court as an entity unto itself with no comparable branch to limit its power or decisions imposed on every other branch of government whether federal or state in the country. The only recourse of the other branches for decisions which they dislike, is to pass new legislation reflecting what they would desire, or, for the President to select nominees of whom he approves as candidates who share his political philosophy. Most of the Presidents have been astounded by the changed outlooks which, over time, have been undertaken by their Supreme Court nominees.

In the current political climate of the United States comprised of radical conservatives (Tea Party Members), large numbers of unemployed persons among middle and lower classes, a growing prevalence of questioning the background of the first black President, and the deadlock of the two major parties unable to compromise and work for the majority interests of the American public, we need to focus upon issues of primary concern for all segments of American society. Without the ability to work across part lines, we face a greater danger than most of our current dissidents seem to realize. Unless there is the ability to compromise on legislative issues stalemate, anger, antagonism and revolts have occurred in other countries which have gone through a similar set of legislative conundrums. The upper class cannot control the future of this country without incurring the wrath of the poor who will see themselves exploited and alienated by those who seem to have everything while the majority of their compatriots feel they have nothing! Should unemployment continue to grow and more and more people left without the means to maintain their families, standard of living and see prospects of improving their lives through their own efforts, as non-existent, our future is bleak at best and politically uncertain and chaotic at worst! The various revolutions in other parts of the world have all begun from the basic cleavage between the wealthy and the forgotten poor. When objection is raised to the reinstitution of taxes upon the upper five percent of our population while reducing them for the other ninety-five percent, we are as close to the edge of revolution as we have ever come. It is, therefore, necessary to consider what the political future of the United States is for the foreseeable future if the conservative radicals should succeed in seizing power! In listening to the descriptions of persons who are asked the question, what do you expect of government, the Tea Party members continue to voice sentiments which indicate 1) they do not know the purpose of government; 2) they cannot think of what government is for and why it exists; 3) their limited ability to pick up on words such as socialism or "Big Government" to castigate what they do not know; 4) they do not realize how utterly dependent they are on the various levels of government for their everyday existence; or 5) they accept the words of persons who seem to speak glibly about the subject of which they obviously know little! Hence, this attempt to help persons to reassess what seems to have been lost, not known, or rejected simply because it seems too far removed from their day to day concerns.

First, as citizens of the United States we should know that federal government exists to secure the common defense. If a country is attacked by another country, there seems to be no hesitation on the part of the general population their only collective cooperation, sacrifice and acceptance of many "hardships" are required to protect the country from being taken over by an attacking nation-state. Private concerns, interests, and property are set aside for the survival of the country. Without any limit on sacrifices and hardships, the defense and success in defeating an attacking country is accepted by the population.

Second, the federal government exists to provide assistance to persons whose lives or property have been subjected to natural disasters over which the population has no control. This aspect of government seems to be universally accepted by the rank and file members of the population of any country, including the United States. The scale of destruction imposed upon the population by such an event imposes its own restrictions on the reservations which persons may have had prior to such a catastrophic event. The immediate goal is to render whatever assistance is required to alleviate human suffering and rebuild what has been lost.

Prof. Donald F. Megnin, Ph.D.

Third, the federal government exists to provide a stable currency and the means for commerce to take place among all persons within the country's borders. Without such a guaranteed access to such funds, only a barter economy would exist. Persons would have to exchange goods based on what the two goods' holders would be willing to accept from the other for the product which each person desired from the other.

Fourth, the federal government exists to provide oversight and regulation of monetary exchanges in order to prevent a monetary collapse of the economy. Banks, businesses, and enterprises all depend upon the orderly exchange of currency, stocks, bonds and values established and fixed by the government so that new businesses, factories, and human activity have been duly recognized as contributing to the growth of wealth and income to the population. Without governmental regulation and oversight, such as we've seen non-existent as recently as 2008, honest transactions could not continue to take place. Legality and honesty were replaced by extortion, piracy and the loss of retirement funds by unscrupulous swindlers who preferred to enrich themselves at the expense of their fellow Americans.

Fifth, the federal government exists to promote the welfare of its citizens through a system of gainful employment leading to a guaranteed retirement upon reaching an agreed upon age at which time it is no longer required of an employee to work because he/she has a system covering retirement costs through the federally funded social security system. This program has been paid for by the retirees themselves through their active years of employment and their contributions made monthly to this retirement fund. This program was first started by the

German government under Chancellor Otto von Bismarck in 1883. It only reached the United States in 1935.

Sixth, the federal government exists to provide health care to all of its citizens through their monthly contributions made from the income they receive through their employment. This feature has been long overdue here in the United States. Some of the European governments have had such a program since the 1930s. Others only since the end of World War II. Only a national government has the capacity to provide universal coverage for all of its inhabitants due to the magnitude, volume, and cost of such a system.

Seventh, the federal government exists to provide the funds to develop the infrastructure (roads, highways, bridges, electrical grids, dams and power plants) so that the growing needs of an expanding population can be continued. The volume and cost of such undertakings are far greater than what can be accomplished by any single state, community, or individual. It is only by concerted and united efforts of a national government that such features of economic expansion is possible.

Eighth, the federal government exists to provide for the safety and security of all of its inhabitants within its borders. The government assists the states through grants of money to provide for the employment of policemen, firemen, social workers, counselors and all of the various levels of state and local government necessary to maintain the peace and protection of persons as they go about pursuing their personal goals and objectives throughout the course of their lifetimes. The states have the primary responsibility to cover these costs. The federal government assists with grants for which the states may apply.

Ninth, the federal government exists to provide a judicial system which adjudicates disputes, property conflicts, and the settling of interpersonal quarrels among individuals and groups comprising the make up of local, state and national authorities under a system of accepted laws and jurisdictions. While most of these types of disputes are settled mostly through the state court systems, the federal authorities remain as the final recourse to settle such disputes. Without such a system, it would be impossible to settle controversies amicably and rationally among contending parties.

Tenth, the federal government exists to protect the right of each individual to present his/her thoughts without fear of censure (free speech), bodily harm, or other forms of intimidation for unpopular points of view. Such a system does not exist in totalitarian countries where governments do not wish to entertain criticism of their rulers, laws or policies for fear of generating a movement for more "freedoms" than these rulers are willing to give to their subjects.

Eleventh, the federal government exists to provide funds for the continuation of scientific enquiry in all areas of science affecting the future growth and development of human beings and in exploring the wider ramparts of the universe. We have slipped to the rank of 12th in science and mathematics among the most highly developed countries of the world. It is only by remaining at the top of such educational achievement that a nation-state will be able to continue to excel in all aspects of its human, economic, and social development in the centuries ahead.

Twelfth, the federal government exists to provide the care of those unable to live on their own or whose families are unable to provide for their special needs. Such a system entails programs for various disabilities so that such individuals have the means to live for whatever years are left to them. The system is best exemplified by the veterans administration which provides not only health care, but disability payments for the recipients to continue to live independent lives.

Thirteenth, the federal government exists to provide an electoral system which allows citizens to elect their own public officials in a regular sequence of terms of office which the voters know and recognize in order to vote for their preferred candidate in each scheduled election. This is one aspect which should be changed to a four year term for the Representative in the House and a limit set for a candidate's electioneering to a three month maximum prior to the election and funding supported by public funds. A suggestion might be to limit such funds to a maximum of two hundred fifty thousand dollars for Representatives and one million dollars for Senators. An adjustment should also be made for state and local elections as well. A servant of the public should be one who is elected based upon what he/she knows and not upon how much money has been given to the candidate by special interest groups to assure access by these contributors to the legislator once he/she is elected.

Fourteen, the federal government exists to guarantee equality of opportunity for all persons based upon each person's needs, abilities, and goals so long as they do not harm or restrict the right of others to do the same. Such governmental activities have gradually evolved over the years in the United States whereby differences of race, religion, and country of origin no longer have an influence on limiting the success or failure of individuals in whatever capacity they've felt inclined to serve. The future of each individual is dependent upon his or her own ability and not only their previous condition, status, or position in society.

Fifteen, the federal government exists to maximize the social and economic conditions which allow all individuals to pursue their goals in the context of the freedom of speech, religion, press, or assembly to indicate in public expressions, verbal or written, which enable persons to make their own decisions in private even as they are constrained by local conditions of employment to be part of the public domain of work.

Sixteen, the federal government exists to guarantee the right of each individual to determine for himself/herself whatever the time frame should be in which life it to be lived or fended depending upon the state of heath of the individual after a full discussion has been carried out with the attending physician. At present there is only one state which allows an individual to decide for himself/herself when to terminate their lives. Such a system should also apply to the decision of individuals to determine the right to end a pregnancy in spite of the prevailing opposing views by those who claim their "right" to deny such an act because it is contrary to their religious beliefs. An individual's right to make such a decision should always prevail even if the end result may be termed regrettable or contrary to popular preference. Each person should have the right to decide for himself/herself what is sacrosanct in democracy in which the government maximizes individual freedom granting each person the right to reach whatever level of life he/she is able to attain.

With these caveats in mind, and a job stimulus program on a national scale, the danger of revolution will subside. Once again, the United States will have achieved the goal of universal employment even if it is called socialism or worse. At least those who have not will be able to survive in a world in which riches have been historically favored and the poor have been subjected to a system of continued exploitation.

Head, Heart, Hands

In examining the life of John Wesley we find three main periods throughout his life which seemed to move in progression from one to the other, bringing forth a facet within himself which he probably never knew existed. But there is to be seen within his life this threefold progression which influenced not only his faith, but the development of Methodism itself. In this progression we note a movement which is consistent within the life of each of us and should become part of our growing experience as time goes on.

Notice, for example, the first period with his life..... the period in which the head predominated. He grew up in a home atmosphere where matters of the mind were of first rate importance. Each of the Wesley children learned to read at age five and had school hours in the home from 9-12 and from 2-5 p.m. each day. Their mother was a strict but fair woman who sought only that her ten surviving children (out of 19) received the best care, discipline and learning that she could give them. Little wonder then that from out of this training ground John should go to Oxford University where he obtained the best that British education could give a young Englishman in the 18th century. He went on to graduate with high honors and was elected to a fellowship as a lecturer of Greek. He later received his Master's degree and dwelled in this atmosphere of a high intellectual for several years. The period of the head predominated in these years of his youth and young adulthood.

In the second period of his life the heart was to predominate. The most dramatic experience of this phase was certainly on the evening of May 24, 1738 when at Aldersgate Chapel he felt his heart strangely warmed. And after this confrontation in which he felt touched by God himself, John Wesley was to write after his Aldersgate experience "I have now peace with God…..In a word, my heart, which before was tossed like a troubled sea, was still and quiet and in a sea of calm." His restlessness had been stilled.

He had gained the assurance of the heart that his faith was real and vital…..that he no longer felt what he believed was empty of accomplishment…..that he now knew the rarity of the fruits of faith as a calm and stilled heart which gave courage and strength to his faith and thought. This was the transition period then of dry intellectualism to the religious period of the heart.

The third period was the period of the hands. With his intellectual understanding of the causes of England's social problems, with his heart felt feeling for the needs of the poverty stricken, the debt ridden and the general abuse of persons and the low regard for human dignity that was so prevalent in England in the 18th century, the grappling with these problems came with the founding of societies of committed Christians; carrying on poor relief with distributions of food, clothing and financial assistance; the founding of schools, chapels, cells of concerned Christians wherever there was interest…..these were all expressions of the diligent use of his hands furthering the work of the Christian Church.

For John Wesley, then, his life represented a constant progression and movement from head, to heart, to hands. On this occasion then, where some persons have joined the church, and more of them are to be installed as officers of this church, and where all of the members of this church need to review their relationship to the Church, notice how we too need to follow this pattern of head, heart and hands as we consider our relationship to the Church as members, officers and officials of this Church.

There is in this pattern of John Wesley's life, first, the necessity of training. This is the use of the mind and intellect to prepare for the assumption of larger responsibilities to which all of us have been called. Training is a necessity these days, and calls for the finest we can obtain in order to carry on our tasks.

At a recent meeting one of the members of our church suggested having training on calling techniques in order to carry on a fall campaign that would be helpful and do some good to know how available it is to those participating. This is taking a step in the right direction. It's a recognition of the necessity of training.....of the use of the mind, before a project of this sort is undertaken.

In Norbert Weiner's book, "Ex-Prodigy: My Childhood and Youth" he writes "Any person with a genuine intellectual interest and a wealth of intellectual content acquires much that he only gradually comes to understand fully in the light of its correlation with other related ideas.....nothing is left in isolation.....each idea becomes a commentary on many others." With training there is a far greater possibility of recognizing the relationship of ideas to one another; of how to relate the mind to body; the head to the heart.

The second pattern that we find in Wesley's life is sensitivity. This is the influence of the heart upon what is seen. Without this sensitivity to the needs and problems others have we cannot begin to utilize our training. This is why it's so hard for the intellectual, the highly trained person to be an effective person in his/her relationship with others. He/she becomes the egghead, the idea person, the one who appears to hold himself/herself aloof from the others. His/her world is one of theory and abstraction. He/she may lack that something extra.....that quality which recognizes the essential humanity of all people including himself/herself. The sensitivity may be lacking. He/she may not know how to be related to his/her heart, to his/her head and still feel like an effective person.

The Duke of Wellington is supposed to have made the comment once, "If you divorce education from religion you will produce a race of clever devils." There's a great deal of truth in that comment. If you divorce the head from the heart you produce as cold and calculating a type of personality as any of the many brilliant men who participated in Nazi scientific experiments or who produced the nuclear weapons in the Soviet Union, Great Britain or in our own United States! Insensitivity alone. allows the heart to temper the mind so that it does not remain cold, indifferent, or cruel to the needs of suffering humankind.

The third pattern that we find in the life of Wesley and one which we should likewise strive to implement is action. James speaks of this quality as "A doer that acts." There's no waiting....there's no thinking, well I'll get it done sometime. "I'll get around to calling that meeting sometime before the end of the summer. I'll have to call on that old neighbor some time.....What a word..... Sometime! It's a word that means "At some time not known or specified." So indefinite that it becomes entirely meaningless. I have to admit, I become very self-conscious whenever I use it. In fact, I try to avoid it as much as possible because I know that once it has been used, the chances of "sometime" becoming this time, the active now is very remote!

One of the finest tributes that the late Pope John XX!!! received was the frequent commendation of his active interest in working with all men of good will for the sake of peace and justice no matter who they were. He revolutionized a church that had for centuries remained implacable toward anyone who was a non-catholic and yet currently he had opened the doors of Catholicism so wide that the breeze of change has blown through the long corridors of the centuries which may keep the door permanently open to the conversation with other religions with whom the Catholic Church would have had no relationship at all just a few years ago!

John Wesley said to every man, if your heart be right give me your hand. In Stringfellow Barr's book "Citizens of the true World" he tells of a young American who spent six weeks working in a Marxist Collective settlement in Galilee, Israel. He met Dr. Martin Buber, the great Israeli philosopher and theologian and asked him "In your writings you are deeply religious. You also see hope of regeneration through the collective settlements, But many of the collective settlements are militarily atheistic. Isn't this a kind of paradox?" "I can answer you," replied Dr. Buber, "Only from a quotation from the Talmud. Would that they had forgotten My name and done that which I commanded of them."

Training, experience and action are the qualities which relate the head to the heart and find expression through the hands!

Can He Walk Without Falling?

In Ralph W. Sockman's book "The Meaning of Suffering" the basic point that he makes is that suffering is a fundamental part of life with variations of suffering facing us constantly. Humans cannot avoid contact with it wherever human beings live. In reference to the home and family living he asks this very basic question "How would a child learn to walk without some falls?"

It's a basic question of life, isn't it? It's impossible to learn without some necessary contrary experience sprinkled in which is a favorable or rewarding experience. It took me quite some time to learn that a parent isn't being cruel and hard who ignores his child after he's fallen down or taken a tumble of some sort. I used to think it was the height of indifference and cruelty when I heard a parent say to his child, "Did you hurt the floor?" after the child had fallen down. I still wouldn't say this, but at least the parent was trying to have the child learn that he should not only feel sorry for himself/herself, but that he should be expecting something like this to happen on occasion and not to feel he's been mortally wounded every time he/she falls. The child has to learn this necessary lesson of life that doing something worthwhile means taking risks, involves difficulties, results in occasional hard knocks.

In the 12th Chapter of John, the 24th verse Jesus says exactly as much when he said, "Unless a grain of wheat falls unto the earth and dies, it remains alone; but if it dies, it bears much fruit." A seed has to die, it has to empty itself by taking root in the soil before it can produce fruit. It has to fall before it can fulfill itself.

I'm not suggesting that we have to die necessarily to give life to others, although in one final sense all of us do this. We have to learn even within our own lifetimes the necessity of taking difficulties, hardships, even falls in our stride.

On the occasion of this mother's day and in conclusion of national family week, I should like to have us examine for a few moments the basis ingredients of family living that we ought to keep in mind. I find in too many families the attempt being made to avoid hardships or difficulties or where parents are trying to shield their children from any contact with risk or possible failure because they believe they are honestly doing their children a favor. And yet, one of the primary necessities of growth is the ability to handle defeat or failure constructively and maturely without allowing the experience to crush us or overwhelm us and make us retreat and seek the comfort and safety of a home we should have outgrown.

The first ingredient of simply living that we ought to keep in mind is its limits. What we have today, we should be able to give up tomorrow, There's an inherent temporariness in family living that many people fail to observe. The small, inner circle of parents and children will inevitably be broken. Life does not allow us to remain forever as we are. The tightest, closest family ties will one day be severed.

In the 1920's Sidney Howard wrote a play entitled "The Silver Cord" in which he demonstrated the turmoil that results in the lives of people who cannot severe the umbilical cord, the silver cord which binds them as children to their families. They do not realize what they have today has to her given up tomorrow. Mrs. Phelps, the mother in the play, had centered her whole life around her two sons. She had been widowed at the age of 25 and her first duty had always been to them. She had never had much romance or love in her life from her husband before he died. And she felt she had gotten it by caring for her two sons. The bankruptcy of this point of view became apparent when the mother and daughter-in-law came to a confrontation and the older married son had to choose between his wife and his mother. He finally chose his wife. The mother was beside herself because she thought she had been betrayed by her son. She took comfort in the fact that she still had her younger son, Robin. "I must remember that I still have one of my great sons. I must keep my mind on that." She turned to this son who was kneeling beside her and the author has her saying to him "And you must remember that David, in his blindness, has forgotten. That mother suffereth long and is kind; envieth not, is not puffed up, is not easily provoked; beareth all things; believeth all things; hopeth all things; endureth all things…..At least, I think my love does?" And Robert, engulfed forever, says, "Yes, mother. They never know what they have today, they could have to give up tomorrow!"

I'm always amazed with the frequency with which parents try to relive their lives in their children. I'm sure they do not realize what they are doing but because of personal frustration or youthful disappointment with their own dreams they seek to avoid the same mistakes in the lives of their children. They never allow their children the right to become independent individuals capable of making their own decisions and living through their own mistakes.

At a recent meeting, we heard one man say how important it was to help children and youth to appreciate the values of education and to put into their minds the automatic thought that they should go to college after high school. This goal would then become second nature to them. What his man did not seem to realize was the fact that he was projecting his own goals upon his children. He had had a hard time getting a college education and he definitely wanted his children to go to college. He was already conditioning them to go the path he had chosen for them. What if his children were incapable of doing this kind of academic work? What if their own search for independence and self identity took them out from the overwhelming burden of their parents' attempt to relive their lives through them? What both this man and woman may have had to realize was that what they had today, they would have to give up tomorrow? We cannot allow ourselves to attempt to relive our own lives through that of our children! They must be allowed to develop their own talents and interests, take their own risks in seeking an understanding of themselves and a knowledge of their own identity.

The second ingredient of family living that we ought to keep in mind is its lessons. From each experience there may be something to be learned. This is a very had concept to accept at times, particularly when the circumstances seem so unfortunate. Do you remember the stories that appeared in the papers in the early sixties about the Thalidomide babies born without fully developed arms and legs? We had one of them studying at the university where I taught years ago. The deformities resulted from the sleeping-pill tranquilizer Thalidomide being taken by the mothers in their early stages of pregnancy. Many couples found this experience too overwhelming to face. Some had even gone so far as to have abortions rather than accept what they felt would be totally handicapped children who would have to be carried around in baskets. Other prospective parents felt it would be too heavy a burden upon their families. What the doctors found out, however, after providing them with artificial limbs they were generally above average in intelligence. Dr. Gustav Hauberg of Hanover and his colleagues were already theorizing about "some mysterious process of natural compensation." When one accepted asset was taken away, another took its place. Even the hardest and seemingly worst experiences provided something from which new insights could be learned.

A mother told me years ago during this episode "I think when one thing is taken away from a person, the Lord provides him with something else." She had seen how this had worked in the life of their son. When polio restricted the boy's physical prowess and ability he had developed one of the most active and persistently good-natured senses of humor she had ever known! Mind he had. He learned from the experience the overwhelming necessity of humor to see the bright side of things in the midst of what seemed so depressing!

Do you remember the reports that came out of the launching of the submarine, Thresher? One of the positive results that was learned from this launching was the necessity to conduct thorough and exhaustive study of the materials to be used in the construction of submarines before they are launched. Some of the troubles the Thresher had had before its launch was the sea-water valves, made to bring in water to cool the nuclear reactor system had not been closing properly. So many valves were switched around during Thresher's overhaul in one of the simulated dockside emergencies, it took twenty minutes for the subs crew to find the valve necessary to cut off the flow through a "broken" pipe. Yet, in actual diving conditions survival could come only with the crew closing off such a flow within seconds.

The air pressure system had been leaky. To surface in an emergency, a submarine must have high air pressure to blow water from its ballast tanks to give it buoyancy. In a flooding situation, anything less than full pressure would drastically slow down water ejection from the tanks.

Portsmouth workers had installed twenty degrees of the hydraulic system valves backwards, inspected and approved their handiwork in that condition. The plane and rudder mechanisms that controlled the dive and cruising angles were still being appraised the night before the submarine went out to sea.

Perhaps from this tragic experience there may have been learned the necessity of sound workmanship and thorough testing and checking before another sub was taken to sea by her crew who could not repair the faulty work of others which was assumed to have been done!

The third ingredient of family living that we ought to keep in mind is its love. We need have no fear of falling. It's a sad fact but a true one, the moral failure, the fear of not meeting the standards imposed by the world upon us has a much greater grip upon Christians today than ever before. And yet our very faith is grounded in the unshakable belief that we have nothing to fear. Take this matter of the fear of failure among students.

Prof. Donald F. Megnin, Ph.D.

In the New York Times magazine section several years ago there was an article entitled "Why of many students flunk out?" The sub-heading summarized the substance of the article very well. "Though high in ability and carefully selected, more and more college students fail to survive through immaturity, family pressures and social distraction." But notice what the author wrote about the failure in the life of the college student. "For most failing students, the hard experience of failure was due to a painful but necessary first step in learning what an education is all about, provided the student, his parents and his college are prepared to join forces in making it so." Just because marks are not so good or even receiving a letter requesting withdrawal from the college because of poor scholarship need not be a mark of total defeat and ignominious failure!

Many years ago a good friend of mine received two f's in his freshman year in college and was asked to withdraw. He was embarked upon a liberal arts course which his family strongly wanted him to pursue. There had been teachers in his family for generations and they thought he was another member who would carry on the family's tradition. Fortunately, the boys's minister recognized his lack of interest in becoming a teacher and helped him enroll in Business Administration. The boy not only went through business administration, but law school as well and today he has finally retired from his law practice in Syracuse.

Again in the concluding words of the article after an official letter of dismissal had been received by the student. "It may well have been a blessing in disguise. It proved to be the same for so many students who had stumbled on the road toward eventual academic success and personal fulfillment."

We need have no fear of falling for God is a part of each experience we have. Rufus Jones once told the story of how archeologists found a little invalid child which had lain buried in volcanic ash in the ancient Roman city of Pompei for nearly two thousand years! Not only was the little boy found but the body of a woman, probably the mother, a woman of noble family who undoubtedly had had plenty of time to escape and save herself. But instead she had gone back to rescue this helpless, deformed boy and through all these years the mother's arm had lain there underneath this little child she died to save, a mute and yet tender token of deathless love. And then Rufus Jones goes on to say, in greater fashion, through the confusions of the world, the din and noise of our busy and material lives, the darkness and mystery of time and space, the everlasting arms of the love of God are underneath us, and He is with us in our pains, our struggles, our follies, our failures striving to put His image upon us and to make us in fact His children."

We need have no fear of failing. The 23rd psalm puts it…."Surely goodness and mercy shall follow me all the days of my life, and I shall dwell in the house of the Lord, for ever."

As Though A Stranger

Emily Post had an excellent suggestion about our homes for this time of the year.

She had written, "Go through your house sometimes as though you had never been there before. Look it over as though you were a stranger."

It's an excellent piece of advice for all of us especially when we find ourselves caught in the same old rut of living. Doing the same thing day after day; going through the same routine, driving down the same street on our way to work; living in the same house in which out parents or even grandparents lived before us. "Look it over as though you were a stranger."

It's another way of saying, try and put yourself outside of the home in which you live and then try to look at it as objectively as you can. Or put yourself into the position of a person who would come to visit you at your work. What would it be like? What would you see that you never noticed before? What would stand out as an eyesore? What would be complimentary and pleasing in what you saw? What would you want to change or correct and cause you to wonder how in the world could you have let that escape your attention for so long?

Several years ago I remember reading about a man who had a record of firsts. He was the first to cross the Triborough Bridge in New York; the first to cross the golden gate in San Francisco; the first to go through the Holland Tunnel, the first to ride down the Taconic State Parkway; the first to go through the gates of Yankee Stadium for the baseball season; the first to travel on the New York State Thruway after it was officially opened. I'm not suggesting that we pursue such a succession of first, but I am suggesting the necessity of attempting to recapture the spontaneity of the first moment you saw your house; the first view you had of your street; the first day on the job; the first time you realized he or she was the one for you!

In this morning's scripture we heard how David recognized how he and all of his people were virtual sojourners, temporary visitors upon earth and then traveled on. "For we are strangers before thee, and sojourners, as all our fathers were."

We hardly seem to realize anymore that we are like strangers, like sojourners, travelers going through God's world. Our mistakes appears to be that of thinking what we have is ours and ours alone to do with as we will. We grow contented with life. We want it to remain exactly as it had always been, leaving our houses just the way they are; with our jobs, just the way we've always known them to be; with our lives just the way we've grown accustomed to doing and hang things.

There's another part of the scriptures we also seem to overlook or forget which is extremely important: "All this abundance that we have provided for building thee a house for thy holy name comes from thy hand and is all thine own." Even all that we have, and are and do comes from

God. Let us reassess our positions and review our lives in order that we may look at ourselves as strangers, even in the midst of what is most common, familiar and known to us. Lest we make the mistake of thinking the world is ours to do with as we see fit and forget that we are but sojourners, travelers, strangers here for a brief time and then moving on....

Let us first of all, ask ourselves, are we satisfied with out home the way it is, or are we interested in what it may become? Since this is spring and house-cleaning is in full swing, if not already completed, I'm sure some of you men know how you are called upon to move the furniture around before you go off to work. Remember how the living room chairs were placed exactly in the positions you felt they were made to fit? The easy chair where you could sit and watch practically everything that went on in the house. And then when the rooms and rugs have been cleaned you find yourself putting the furniture not back into the old familiar places, but changed around. Your wife reminds you of the necessity of periodic alteration and rearrangement, She not only is looking at the house as though a stranger, but you find yourself feeling like one for a few days until you've become accustomed to the new scheme of things in the house. She's not interested in the house the way it was, but in what it might become!

My wife was talking with a woman a short time ago and she said, "With old houses there's always a lot of work to do. First, you have to fix up one room and then another one doesn't look right so you have to work on that one. The floors are uneven, the ceilings begin to sag. It's just one continuous job after another that has to be taken care of." But isn't this exactly one of the ways in which God does not let us rest? Isn't this another way of reminding us that we cannot be satisfied with our home the way it is, but must continually carry on repairs to demonstrate we are interested in what it will become?

Next to an abandoned person or animal, the thing that evokes the greatest amount of emotion in me is to see an old abandoned house or barn. It's like seeing something dead on the streets. An existing skeleton of what was once alive and healthy, bursting with the energy of people who were not satisfied in letting it remain the way it was, but which was pulsating with the breath of life of what it might become!

This is exactly what happens with slums.....and I would be brazen enough to suggest that if persons or landlords are satisfied with allowing their houses to remain slummy eyesores from which they're only interested in extracting rent from their impoverished victims, their properties should be sold by the victims and their properties purchased by the community or city and a prompt and decent burial accorded by tearing them down. This is what was done years ago in the 15th ward. May I remind you to be careful about allowing the infiltration of two and three family units being established in what are, essentially, one or at most, two family unit dwellings..... It's not that there are no landlords who are interested in keeping up their properties. The point is there are an equal number, I fear more, who are satisfied to leave things just the way they are and who couldn't care less what may become of them! The housing codes are flaunted daily because the rest of us don't seem to object or don't want to start any trouble, or one hundred and one excuses are given which later result in our living in a slum where no one seems to care in what their homes become! Are we satisfied with our homes the way they are, or are we interested in what they may become?

Secondly, let us ask ourselves, are we satisfied with out lives the way they are, or are we interested in what they might become? A lot of people make fun of this peculiar doctrine of the Methodist Church about going on to perfection. But is a person isn't going on to perfection, he/she just isn't going, period! A person's life has to have a state of motion to it. It's not necessarily a motion of physical movement, but a move into areas of experience you've never tried before…. Anyone who has ever served on a nominating committee knows the type of replies people make when they're asked to hold an office or a position for the coming year. "Oh, I couldn't do that! I don't know enough to take on that kind of responsibility. You'd better ask someone else; someone who's more qualified than I am."

It's amazing how many people aren't interested in any motion of any kind. They seem to be satisfied with their lives exactly as they are. Not at all interested in what they might try to experience, might try or utilize to the thrill of doing something they've never done before…..the experience of seeing what they might become!

I wonder if I may speak for a moment to those of you who are getting a little older than the rest of us. Keep motion a part of your day's activity as long as possible. Don't fall into the habit that some of my contemporaries have gotten into of lethargy and inactivity which is making them old years before their time!

It was Dr. Paul Dudley White, the heart specialist of Boston whose fame increased with the care of former President Eisenhower after his heart attack who used to ride around the streets of Cambridge each morning on his bicycle. He not only advocated this type of physical activity, but he insisted upon it and carried it out even though he was in his late seventies.

There's a woman in this parish who's a most unusual woman and one who wasn't satisfied to let age keep her from seeing what she might become. Do you know what she does each day? She climbs the stairs of house everyday so that when Sunday morning comes, she can climb the stairs of our church and worship with us as she had done for more years than probably most of us will ever see.....

She fulfills the meaning of the words David spoke "Keep forever such purposes and thoughts in the hearts of thy people, and direct their hearts toward thee."

Are we satisfied with our lives the way they are, or are we interested in what they might become? Practically every person who has been to Africa comes back to tell us that the most impressive impression they have about the African peoples is their overwhelming interest in learning; in getting an education; in dissatisfaction with their lives the way they are and their sincere desire to see what they can become!

It's terrible but true, when we have little we are apt to realize how important something is, while when we have a great deal, we forget what is most important. Materialism does stand in our way. We are prone to lose sight of the necessity of the work and sacrifice that went into providing what we have. Take this matter of television. It could be one of the greatest opportunities for cultural understanding and educational broadening available to human beings! But what do we find it primarily used for in America today? Entertainment! With a heavy sprinkling of advertising likewise entertainingly thrown in!

My wife tells me she heard one of you describe television as "the worst nemesis that's ever hit America!" It's unfortunately true. It's geared to the lowest common denominator. And when we are not selective in what we see, we remain upon the lowest denominator of satisfaction with our lives exactly the way they are, and lose all sense of understanding of what we might become…..We lose sight of a view of our lives as though a stranger who tries to "Keep forever such purposes and thoughts in the hearts of thy people, and direct their hearts toward thee."

And finally, are we satisfied with the world as it it, or are we interested in what it might become? The complacency and smug self-satisfaction about life is overwhelming to behold. It makes you wonder where in the world have they person been for the past human history? What goes on today has been going on for centuries and it is anything but a picture of complacent satisfaction that can be derived from it. A poet, Sara Henderson Hay looking at modern life saw ancient Biblical characters all over again and wrote:

"Stones crumble, but more staunchly fares

A dust incredibly translated:
Judas still haggles at his wares,
Cain is forever newly created.
Delilah, in a Paris frock,
Goes out to tea at 5 o'clock:
Salome clubs the subway stairs,
Potiphar takes the elevated."

The world is anything but something over which to become complaisant, or smugly satisfied.

George Bernard Shaw is supposed to have made the comment that "the Bible is more up to date than the morning newspaper….." I would alter it to say the morning newspaper is simply the Bible brought up to date…..The same characters exist today as they did then.

Halford Luccock told of seeing a man make a brilliant 200 yard dash in New Haven that would have broken all records if he had been timed in order to catch the bus Dr. Luccock was riding. And when he caught it the question he asked was "Where's the bus going?" That's just about the way most of us appear to be dealing with the reality in which we find ourselves. Except, even after we've made a brilliant run, we don't even ask the question of what our destination is or stop to consider whether we want to go there or not.

Are we satisfied with life as it is, or are we interested in what it might become? If we're satisfied with the world as it is then what about the increasing problem of racial strife that's breaking out in various cities of this country? What about the increasing problem of crime practically at the doors of our own university? What about the increasing problem of run down neighborhoods, blight areas where crime breeds and people subjected to the indifference of neighbors who don't care soon lose any interest in the welfare of their neighborhood and can no longer control and limit the invasion of commercial, industrial and liquor interests which are interested in profits first, property second, and people in last place?

Still satisfied with the world the way it is? Then what about the increasing problem of our aging society which has too little medical care for fear of losing a lifetime of savings or of becoming a ward of the public? Such may be the future if the Republican controlled Congress decides to cut off the Obama Health Care program which was passed last year! What about the increasing problem of food surpluses in a world that's close to starvation? What about the problem of the spread of nuclear weapons among first one than two, then three, four and soon five, six or a dozen different countries?

Still satisfied with the world just the way it is? Then I invite you to look at your home, your life, and the world as though a stranger through the impartial eyes of God and let us see what we can do to "Keep for ever such purposes and thoughts in the hearts of thy people, and direct their hearts toward thee" and create the world as it might become.

It Depends On How It Is Used!

In Alfred Noyes' Poem, "The Torch-Bearers" he describes Galileo showing his new the telescope to the Senators of Florence.....and the old men say to one another

"This glass will give us great advantages in time of war!"

Presented by science with a gift that could expand the mind and spirit of man, these old men thought first of "great advantages in time of war." And the poet cries out

"O God of love,
Even amidst their wonder at they world,
Dazed with new beauty, gifted with new powers,
These old men dreamed of blood!"

There you have it, the opportunity to view the universe in all its awe and splendor. and yet their thoughts turned to war! From the simplest tool to the most complex space vehicle; from the humblest life to the greatest by world acclaim, the value of each item depends upon how it is used! Look around this morning. There is nothing which you and I can see that does not have within it the potential for good or evil depending upon how it is used! A book thrown across a room can strike someone a fatal blow;

a chair upended may cause someone a fatal fall; a piano tipping over could crush someone beneath it. But you say this couldn't happen......This is rather far fetched, a book isn't going to go flying across a room or a chair isn't going to be tipped over, or a piano isn't going to tip over on anyone! Then you don't know what small children are capable of or the dangers oldsters are subject to!.

Consider your trip here this morning. Think of how you or someone else might have used their car, not as a comfortable means of transport, but as a vehicle of injury or death. It's not as far fetched as you might think for anything we have, or are which may be used for good or evil depending upon how it is used!

When Alfred Nobel invented dynamite in 1867, he believed so terrible an explosive would never be used in war! He saw it as a tremendous advantage for harnessing nature for man's benefit. Leonardo da Vinci, on the other hand. designed a submarine, but tore up the plans for fear of what men might do with it!

Some years ago a Clergyman's Day was held at the Air Force Base at Hancock Field. We were taken through that mysterious looking concrete building at the base and the mystery of what was in it was replaced by an incredible array of data concerning our radar computer defense systems guarding the North American continent from polar attack. Every aircraft could be followed from one end of this country to the other, if necessary and identification could be checked in a matter of a few minutes. It was a truly marvelous system of watching and guiding air craft in order to achieve safety for the growing numbers of the flying public.

It was also a rather frightening prospect of how it might be used if an object should ever be identified as unfriendly. We were told over 300 B-52 bombers of the Strategic Air Command would be in the sky in a matter of minutes to deliver 20 megaton nuclear bombs to the enemy. In a matter of hours, more than 50 million Russians would be killed…..to say nothing of the tens of millions of Americans that would be killed in the event of such an attack. A tremendous achievement of man in providing safety, but also a terrible means of destruction should the signals of this sort indicate danger. The value of our institutions, our instruments and implements, our resources, our lives depend upon how they are used!

How shall we view these possibilities? Should we view them with alarm? If everything has such a potential of danger to us why even carry on any further? A lot of people feel that way at times…..

They feel life is just too dangerous to continue and they either try to withdraw from it and retire into isolation or end it completely in suicide. Reading the accident statistics brings us up against the fact that more accidents take place in the home than anywhere else. And suicide is hardly an answer to the problem of adjusting to circumstances we may not like. It's a pretty final decision from which there is no recourse.

Instead of being overwhelmed by the possibility of danger that lurks about us, let us not forget that danger can not only be a source of fear but of faith. As on educator put it, "Education consists in being afraid at the right time." There's no doubt about the fact that this is a time to be afraid. We cannot take our civilization for granted any more…..We can lose it…..One more war with nuclear weapons and it'll be gone! Of course there's danger. Of course there's fear, but this kind of danger may be a constructive incentive to notable achievement. Look at our schools. Behind them is the fear of illiteracy and ignorance but also the faith that these problems may be overcome through education. Look at our medical science and hospitals, behind them is the fear of insufferable pain and diseases, but also the faith that these maladies will be alleviated through research and constant care. Look at our churches, synagogues and temples, behind them is the fear of the unknown, the utter possibility of loneliness and the meaninglessness of life, but also the faith that God cares for his children and seeks for them as they do for him.

Danger is not only a source of fear, but of faith as well. It is said of that great Portuguese sailor, Henry the Navigator, that neither he not his men feared of anything. Yet they could not free themselves from the superstitions which characterized their age. Their charts revealed their fear of danger for on them since there were vast unexplored wastes over which the geographers had written the weird legends, "Here be dragons. Here be demons. Here be sirens." A British navigator, later to become Sir John Franklin, knew no more of those unknown regions than his earlier fellow-navigators. There was an entire hemisphere into which he had never penetrated. However, when these charts came into his hands he crossed out the superstitions and boldly wrote in their place, "Here is God."

It depends on how danger is used. It need not only be a source of fear, it may also become a source of faith as well.

Perhaps people are afraid of change. They feel threatened by the new demands which may be made upon them. They feel satisfied and comfortable with themselves. They do not think about the future of either themselves or anyone else.They want to feel their way into the future. That is, they want to do as they have always done, as they please. And then when any change is introduced, if anything is done differently than in the past, they react to the change. They resist it. They resent it. Change means for them conflict. They forget what we must not forget, change means not only conflict, but can mean creativity as well! Let me make a little confession of my own concerning change. I sometimes resent it and resist it like anyone else, especially if it invokes Saturdays! Very often my wife and I are invited for a Saturday evening, or to a wedding and reception on a Saturday afternoon. Whenever I hear about a Saturday engagement of some sort, I just bristle! Don't people realize that's the day sermons are finished? The time when the minister likes to lock himself away from everyone until his sermon is finished? But now and then someone will call. They just have to talk to the minister that afternoon! It can't wait! A sudden change in my weekly schedule and I'm just as grouchy and grumpy as any one else if I forget the creativity possible within these moments of contact. The miracles of mood may be cast in those moments of contact in counseling or in a marriage celebration. The difference in attitude on the part of the persons involved may be made by what you say or do.

This is the opportunity of any change, the creativity of seeing something in a new light; of participating in the formulation of a new idea or plan; of inspiring confidence, that courage to act is essential to a free and decisive personality.

You know as well as I that change is viewed too often in terms of conflict….that new ideas or plans are resented and resisted not because of their merits, but because people are unwilling to live creatively. They view life as having to be made pleasing unto themselves instead of making themselves pleasing unto life!

Reginald Reynolds who wrote the book "From Cairo to Cape Town" where he suggested changes that must be made in the privileges held by Europeans in predominantly African lands in self-defense wrote a parable after hearing altogether too often that an outsider couldn't judge the inside of a situation: "A certain man coming into a room where a number of people had been sitting for some hours, remarked that the room was stuffy.

The people sitting there were very annoyed at his remark. How can you presume to judge asked one man, when you have only this minute come in?"

Another said: "It is always these people from outside who make this ill informed criticism. Only those who have sat here for hours can possibly know whether the air is fresh or foul! It is just to keep out ignorant critics like you, said a third, that we keep all the doors and windows shut! So they threw the intruder out and bolted the door!"

Ladies, as your minister, before you decide to throw the intruder out, I'd suggest opening some of the windows of your faith that have been closed through the years by the restrictive leadership in your circles and classes and let the fresh winds of change sweep through your lives to invigorate them in order to let your sleeping talents of creative leadership become aroused and alive to new possibilities of thought and action after all of these years of sleep and faithful obedience to exploiting your old friends! Yes, the value of change is dependent upon how it is used!

One final word must be said not only about the constructive use of danger and the creativity of change, but of the very value of life itself determined by its use. If a man says, "I love God" and hates his brother, he is a liar. If he does not love the brother before his eyes how can he love the one beyond his sight? Many people attempt a mental divorce between what they see and what they want to believe.

The Russian communists on the eve of their great revolution literally threw themselves into the righteousness of their cause with a wholeness of conviction and courage that absorbed all of their energies, talents, and lives in the cause of ridding their people of the yoke of oppression and exploitation. There was no distinction to be made between their ideals and their lives. They were truly one! It was only later, after the success of their cause that the discrepancy between what they believed and did became apparent. There were not many communists who would admit that there was or is a discrepancy between what they did and what they believed. In fact, there are not many persons at anytime who ever see the discrepancy in their own lives between what they believe and what they do!

Probably the most graphic examples we can think of are the War Crimes' Trials of Japanese and German government leaders at the end of World War II. None of them, not a one felt the least regret for anything they had done. They saw no discrepancy between what they did and the orders they maintained that all men must follow in obedience to the interests of their countries. The only regret they had was they had lost the war. Even Adolph Eichman claimed he was merely a ticket agent, the tool of a chain of command over which he had no control. And Eichman was, in a sense on trial for each of us. He was condemned to death for not willingly taking the cross of death himself in the face of what he saw and knew to be evil. all of us are just as guilty as he if we refuse to recognize the value of a life comes from how it is used…..The only difference is that probably none of us will ever be brought to trial for it. We'll get by as a person. It's only later that someone looking back at this age in history will say, there were few who saw the relationship between life and its use as an instrument of God.

> "Take my life and let it be
> Consecrated Lord to Thee
> Take my moments and my days
> Let them flow in ceaseless praise.
> Take my hands and let them move
> At the impulse of they love.
> Take my feet, and let them be
> Swift and beautiful for Thee."

Dialogue With Diversity

Lloyd George, British Prime Minister during World War I had the task, as a boy, of collecting firewood in the nearby forest for the kitchen stove where the cooking was done and which also provided the warmth for their house. When the days were sunny and bright he had endless hours for play and other childhood delights in the out of doors. But on the bright sunny days, it was difficult to find the branches and sticks needed for the stove. On days when it rained and stormed, he could mot go out to play, but had to stay inside the house. After the storms passed, however, when he went outside after firewood there was plenty to be found and taken home.

It was only years later that Lloyd George recognized the meaning of what had happened. While the sun was shining he had lots of opportunity to play, but when he went after firewood he couldn't find much…..The dead trees and limbs simply blended into the rest of the forest of living things, but after a storm, he had no difficulty in finding more than enough wood than he needed. Although the storms had prevented him at the time from playing out of doors, the wind and storm had swept through the forest tearing off branches, knocking over dead trees and generally separating the living from the dead. It was only under the pressure of the storm that the shaking out of the deadwood was possible. Through the dialogue of fair and foul weather he realized the gain where he once thought there was only loss. He saw that not only sunny skies but stormy weather had value. There is in life a constant dialogue going on between opposites.....and for each one of us there is a constant dialogue going on not only with opposites, but with diversity.

In the sermon which I preached recently, it may have appeared that I sounded extremely harsh toward those persons with whom we may disagree.....that I was being unfair with anyone who may have legitimate opposing views, perhaps even within this church. I should like to state categorically there would be nothing so lethal to the growth of this church. I should like to state categorically there would be nothing so lethal to the growth of this church or any human institution than the suppression of opposition. We need opposition.....We should encourage difference of opinion. In fact, we should encourage difference for the sake of difference itself.....for the sake of humankind; for our own sakes!

The cultivation of diversity is as necessary as the process of smelting is to the purification of any ore..... different ingredients have to be added before the essential metal is obtained in its purified form.

We as a nation have long been called the melting pot of the world; people from all over the world with a wide variety of different cultures, with different customs and laws have maintained the unity of common interests despite the wide diversity of backgrounds. In theory our democratic system of government calls for unity through diversity and before this unity can take place a dialogue between opposites or among differences must ensue!

Through a constant dialogue with diversity truth can be discovered; justice carried out; and goodness affirmed! Let us examine some of the ways in which we carry on this dialogue each day; ways in which we may not even be conscious of how it is taking place.

There is, first of all, the daily dialogue we have with our environment. Will I get up this morning and prepare breakfast for you husband/wife, or won't I? Will I get up in the morning and go to work, or won't I? Will I get up in the morning and go to school today or won't I?

These are all questions in the daily dialogue we have with our environment. So long as we move, breathe, or undertake any action at all, we are a part of this dialogue.

Many years ago two friends and I were standing on the shores of Lake Michigan watching the waves pound against the shore and then sweep out again. One of them said, "You know, these waves and the endless sweeping back and forth of the water reminds me of how timeless life really is. Nothing ever really changes…..It's the same thing over and over again…..Just like this water" The other friend listened and looked at the waves for a while and then he said, "I think what you've said is exactly how most of us sometimes feel….That nothing ever seems to change…..but that's just the secret of it…..Even as we think so and watch the action of the waves, there's a great deal of change going on….. The very bank we're standing on will probably end up in the bottom of this Lake in years to come…..With each sweep of the waves on the shore literally millions of grains of sand, rock, and soil are being moved even though we're unaware of it. These waves show me how really creative and different life can be."

Each day is a dialogue between life and ourselves. Life asks you, are you going to meet the challenges of work, study, of home today, or not? We answer by how we do our job…..by how we do our homework, by how we prepare our meals or put the house in order.

The second dialogue is the one we have with one another. It may be with our wife or husband…..It may be with our son or daughter who lives with us…..It may be with a friend…..It may be with our neighbor or the man on the street…..It may be with the men at the shop or with the boss…..The dialogue may be with any person….. To recognize that each person is a child of God means each one has the right to express his point of view no matter how much we may disagree with it. No two people have exactly the same experiences…..No two individuals view a given circumstance in exactly the same way…..A poet put it inaptly when he wrote, "Two men were looking through the self-same bars. The one saw the mud, the other, the stars!" We bring to each circumstance an individual variety of experiences and knowledge. We cannot expect each person to view something exactly as we view it…..We are not them and they are not us!

This past week one of the most remarkable events in human history took place, but did you notice the reactions to this event? The same sort of reaction took place when the Russians launched the first manmade satellite. One man immediately rationalized the position of the United States by saying, "The U.S. is still ahead in many fields of science. This is an attempt on the part of the Russians to impress the African nations!" The reaction in Congress was much the same, "We must excellerate our efforts immediately to get a man in space. This Russian success is an indication of how far behind we are in the space race."

The reaction on the part of some of our leaders to discredit this brilliant human achievement of Russian science only calls to mind a story I once heard Alex Carmichel give in a sermon several years ago. He said there was once a convention scheduled in Chicago and many of the hotels were busy getting their houses in order for the delegates' arrival. The doors were polished. The corridors washed and waxed. The rugs sent our for washing. The lounge chairs were scrubbed. The uniforms of the bellhops were cleaned and freshly pressed. Everything was ready for the big day when the hotel manager noticed a rather disheveled looking man sleeping on one of the couches right in the middle of their freshly scrubbed lounge. His hair looked as though it hadn't been combed for a week....... His necktie was twisted and his collar open. His suit was badly wrinkled and looked like pajamas after they've been slept in for a few nights. Despite the rather messy appearance of the man, the manager wasn't sure whether this man was a delegate who had decided to celebrate a little early or whether he was just one of the drunken sots that sometimes stumbled into the hotel and curled up on the couch. He didn't want to take a chance on throwing him out.....He might offend the other delegates if he were one of them....He didn't want to leave him there so that the next morning the arriving delegates would see him and wonder what kind of a hotel they were in.....He just didn't know what to do. He tried waking him and it just didn't work.....He snored on and on. The manager got more and more desperate as the hour approached for the grand opening.....Then one of the bellboys come over to his boss and said he had a sure way of getting rid of the man without doing him or the hotel any harm. The manager said, "You can try anything it it'll work! Just get him out before the delegates arrive."

The bellhops went to the kitchen and got a knife and some limburger cheese. He went over to the man with the knife and put some limburger cheese on the knot of his necktie. The bellhop left confident he would get rid of him…..Pretty soon the drunk on the davenport stirred from his slumber and began to sniff around. He struggled to a sitting position and kept on sniffing, trying to find the spot where the small came from…..He leaned over and looked behind the davenport. He couldn't find anything there…..He got up, lifted the cushions, but couldn't find anything there. He went over to the other chairs and went through each of those sniffing as he went, but he couldn't find anything there. He went to the curtains by the windows, looked behind the large potted plants on the sides of the corridor, looked behind the huge paintings on the wall and sniffed and sniffed. He seemed to find the same stink wherever he looked, but couldn't find the cause of it. He finally stumbled his way toward the door and as he went out of the hotel he said to the bellboy, "The whole world stinks, doesn't it?"

This is just the way we view the world we forget ours is a dialogue with other people not only with those who agree with us politically and culturally, but also with those who may violently disagree with us! So long as we have any discussions at all with another person or persons we carry on a dialogue and their views are as legitimate of expression as are ours.

The third of the daily dialogues we carry on is the dialogue of the individual with society. We are limited in what we can and cannot do according to how our interests conflict with those of others.

When we were serving a church on the north side of Syracuse a neighbor boy used to use our church door as a backstop for his baseball which he kept throwing against these doors and catching it as it bounded back to him. He kept this practice up for some time until my wife went out and asked him to stop using our doors as a backstop. He was perfectly content with this sport, really improving his catching of grounders. The thought never occurred to him that the Church doors were not his private property to do with as he pleased. He wasn't conscious of the fact that he was contributing to the destruction of the building and thereby ruining its use by all of the rest of us. It was an innocently made error and all of us as children had to learn to accept these limitations on our activities in order not to deprive others of their rights. But this is exactly what happens when we cheat on our taxes; when we seek our own profit at the expense of an unsuspecting public.

Did you see that cartoon by Herblock years ago in the Herald-Journal? It showed the long arms of the U.S. public holding by the scruff of their collars two characters of corruption in unions and corruption in government and the other hand holding a magnifying glass on the figure of corruption in business who stood shielding his bags of profit beneath him while pointing up a self-righteous finger saying, "Hold on, now, don't interfere with free enterprise!"

It's about time this was done.....This kind of so-called legitimate "profit-making" is exactly what's going to destroy our system of free-enterprise! The dialogue between the rights of the individual and his responsibility to society is one that some of us seem to forget on occasion and its exactly through this method of probing into what individuals illegally do that we prove is the lie that individual rights do not mean the right of irresponsibility. Each day we carry on this dialogue of what we can do as individuals and what the same rights granted to other persons does not allow us to do. We have the right to learn how to drive a car, but his does not allow us to drive recklessly as if we didn't care what happened to someone else. We have the right to an education, but this does not allow us to withhold this right from those of another race. We have the right of life, liberty, and the pursuit of happiness, but this does not allow us to take liberties with our neighbors. We have the right to love and be loved by other people, but we cannot force our affection upon them. We have the right to get married and raise a family, but we do not abdicate our responsibility of providing for them once we've accepted it. As members of churches, we have the right to expect the best possible care and training of our children in religious education, but do we have the right to demand it when we fail to participate in it ourselves? We have the right to expect that once we've joined a church we shall acquire all of its privileges, but do we have a right to receive what we do not give of our time, talents, and resources?

In Shakespeare's play, Julius Caesar, Casius says to Brutus, "The fault, Dear Brutes, is not in our stars, but in ourselves that we are underlings!" The daily dialogue that takes place between society and ourselves is the one that determines not only how we shall live, but the kind of society we shall have. What you and I do with our rights as individuals makes a difference in the kind of rights we all have in society.

An English preacher by the name of Angus Watson tells the pathetic story of an English Army officer who, during the war, left his quarters one night to consort with a prostitute in a city overseas. He was married but in his frustration at being overseas excused his conduct for the one night even though he did not lapse again…..When he finally returned home at the end of the war the temporary lapse was only a memory to him. A year later his first and only daughter was born, but she was born blind. He had contracted syphilis without knowing it and the seeds of his misdeed had blighted the life of his little girl. Every day as he watched the small groping figure feeling her way about the house, he was reminded again and again of the action that had brought blindness to her. For the rest of his life he could not forget the consequences of his one act......

Each day brings a dialogue to be held between ourselves and society Each day you and I determine what the values shall be for our society by advancing them or destroying them. This is the dialogue we carry on with life itself. This is the dialogue we carry on with another person and between ourselves and the wider society of which we are a part. Each one of these dialogues is a dialogue with diversity which determines not only our neighbor's life, but our own!

That's Where We Came From

After the performance of Thornton Wilder's play, "Our Town", a prosperous New Yorker and his wife, who had evidently grown up in a small town like Grover's Corners were talking about the play coming down the aisle. The play was a simple and impressive picture of a small town in New Hampshire around the turn of the 20th century. An order of life had been shaped by the church and definitely expressed Christian standards and values. The man was overheard saying to his wife, complacently, "Well, that's where we came from baby!" She gave him an unexpected answer, "Yes, and I'm wondering where we've gotten to? You wouldn't catch me living in that town again! Did you notice how strict and quaint they were? Why is it you didn't go to church on Sunday when you were practically run out of town!" Yes, we've certainly made progress since then!

Yes, and I'm wondering where we've gotten? We're living in a big city.....There are few restrictions placed on us of what we can or cannot do.....We can entertain whom we please, when we please, where we please.....We can do just about anything we want. We're part of the freedom of the city.....We're rid of those silly restrictions a little town and a country church exercises over our lives.....We're really free individuals!

"Yes, and I'm wondering where we've gotten....." She was asking for a reappraisal of their lives....of what they considered important.....of what had taken the place of the values of the small town and its church.....?

Where have we gone? What have we accomplished since we left the bygone days of a church controlled community where the standards were clearly understood; where the values for each person were spelled out in unmistakeable terms?

"That's where we came from." And where have we gotten? What has taken the place of the greatest loyalty today?

We've been released from the bonds of superstition, but have we grown in faith? A couple of years ago a group of us took a trip along the New England coast looking over the historical landmarks that had such a heavy influence upon early American history. One of the places we visited was Salem, Massachusetts. What a tragic bit of history this town represented in the late seventeenth century. These New Englanders took for granted the ancient belief that the devil night take residence in human bodies and compel his unhappy hosts to perform all sorts of supernatural evil. In 1692 all Salem was convulsed by hysteria. Deluded or mischievous children screamed and rolled on the ground, accusing one neighbor after another of tormenting them. The accused often confessed either to escape torture or because they fell under the same delusion as their accusers. After nineteen witches had been put to death and the number of suspects began to mount into the hundreds, New England suddenly came to its senses. The setting of the town lent itself to all sorts of fanciful thought. As one rides into it at night from the north, you go through rather swampy scenes mixed with low hills and scattered trees. It has the eerie sort of atmosphere about it even today. But in this setting the evils of witch hunting began.

We've been released from this belief in demons, evil spirits, and witchery but have we become more certain of God's goodness? Visiting a Russian nursery school many years ago, we were impressed with the creative toys and natural wild life scenes that the children could look at around their classrooms. It was almost like a museum. There were books illustrated with pictures for easy visualization of what seas being read to them. But what was most amazing of all was the fact that no fairy tales were either told or read to the children. We were told this would only prove harmful to the children and as they grew to adulthood they would simply have to unlearn all of these fantastic ideas. Better to start from realism and then the children can continue to understand life without being confused and perplexed by finding out what they had once heard was not true.....

I could not help but think about what liberates the mind......that only truth unshadowed, unfiltered, unleashed could really release an individual from living in a dream world of childish unreality and bring him/her to an even greater faith in the goodness of God by seeing life as it really is.

And yet, I fear, we have not yet been fully released from the bonds of myth and superstition. I fear we still confuse myth with fact; superstition for religion; fear for faith. We still find people teaching the myth of creation or of Noah's ark found in the book of Genesis as a fact..... We still find people superstitiously carrying little crosses or statues on their persons or in their cars in the belief that his provides them with good luck and, therefore, they are being religious.....We still find people who pray, pray and pray when they are undergoing some great stress or face some great fear and believe that his represents faith for them. I could not but feel painfully sorry for all of those Cuban mothers, fathers, wives and sweethearts who prayed so diligently that their sons, husbands, and boyfriends would not be hurt during their invasion of Cuba. The churches of Florida were filled by the faithful who prayed for the safety and success of the men on their mission.

Can we look at reality as it really is? Can we shake off the fetters of falsehood and see our responsibility for making of life whatever we will? Can we believe that nothing whatsoever can separate us from the love of God? If we can, we're on the road toward a growing faith.

Secondly, we've been released from the strict religious discipline imposed on us by the church. Have we substituted a private discipline for it in our own lives?

Many years ago, I talked with a woman who said as a girl, her mother never let her miss a Sunday without going to church. She had to go to Sunday school and then to church. She had to go to prayer meetings on Wednesday evenings too. Later she had to sing in the Cherub Choir and then the youth choir. She sort of accepted this weekly program of going to church, that is until she graduated from high school and started working away from home. She said, "You know, I haven't been to a church service since then. Oh, I go to some of the church suppers and annual sales and bazaars, but I haven't missed going to church at all. I learned my prayers as a little girl. I prayed and I know my prayers were answered. I don't need to go to church to be religious. I'm just as religious as the next person."

I couldn't help but think what a rather prosperous New Yorker said to his wife after attending a play, "That's where we came from baby!" And his wife answered, "Yes, and I'm wondering where we've gotten?" I have wondered where she has gotten through all these years of protest and revolt against her mother's forcing her to go to church every week…..Where was the private discipline in her life to take the place of the one she had thrown off like a dirty coat?

It may be a fine and sometimes a necessary idea to throw off the yoke of a harsh and distasteful discipline imposed upon you, but the truth of the matter is, what are you going to put in its place? It's easy to say I resent and renounce the discipline my parents forced on me as a child. It's pretty easy and necessary to say, I'm going to run my life the way I want to from now on, but the hard fact of the matter is, unless we put an even harder private discipline in place of parental discipline, we may again become enslaved to an even worse discipline: the discipline of bad habits!

Shortly after finishing college, I was asked to represent Syracuse University at Chulalongkorn University as a Lecturer of English for Thai students. I shared a house with two other men one of whom was a former Mormon. His childhood had been severely strict and his parents saw to it that he would not be exposed to any influence that would in any way lead him out of the path Mormonism. He was not allowed to drink alcoholic beverages, smoke, swear, or have dates until he was out of high school. World War II was going on by this time and as an eighteen year old he had to go into the Army. For the first time in his life he was out from under the discipline of his strict Mormon parents and society. He maintained his strict Mormon posture for a time, but gradually he felt further and further isolated from the "Thou shalt not" of his parents. Hie religious beliefs came to be viewed as not only a bit weird and odd by his buddies, but he began to wonder how he ever could have believed such strange ideas himself. As he drank of his freedom from the discipline of his parents he also began drinking increasingly of the spirits from which his friends drank. Smoking became a matter of course for him, swearing legitimate expressions of how he really felt and dating became a requirement. When I knew him, the discipline of drink, smoke, and sex had such a hold on him that he could not escape from them. He had accepted an even more tortuous discipline of bad habits in place of those he had revolted against.

While he has been released from the strict religious discipline imposed upon him by his Church, have we accepted the private discipline that makes life worth living? Have we seen how a protest against a way of life must be balanced by an affirmation for a new way of life? Have we recognized the necessity of accepting a standard for life that gives our lives meaning and purpose? If not, then we are still as bound to a discipline of bad habits as we ever were by the imposed Disciples of the Church!

Finally, we have been released from a narrow interpretation of life, but what have we put in its place? We're sort of like little children when it comes to naive views we hold about life's requirements of us. The author, John Ruskin, told of his first lessons he learned as a little boy. "First," he said, "I had to learn what it meant to be obedient. The discipline began early. One evening, when I was yet in my nurse's arms, I wanted to touch the tea-urn, which was boiling merrily. It was an early taste for bronzes, I suppose; but I was resolute about it. My mother bid me keep my fingers back; I insisted on putting them forward. My nurse would have taken me away from the urn; but my mother said, Let him touch it, nurse! So I touched it; and that was my first lesson in the meaning of individual liberty. It was the first piece of liberty I got, and the last which for some time I asked for."

How like this we are…..We would be free to do what we like, to taste what we please, to touch what should be left alone…..The Church is still against drinking. gambling, all human excesses, corruption, injustice, hypocrisy but notice the degree to which we are all engaged in one or more of these vices…..including the Church itself! The Methodist Social Creed maintains freedom from discrimination, "We stand for equal rights of racial. cultural, and religious groups and insist that the social, economic, and spiritual principles set forth in this creed apply to all alike. The right to choose a home, enter a school, secure employment, vote, or join a church should not be limited by a person's race, culture, or religion." And yet the Methodist Church used to maintain in clear contradiction of its own stated goals…..a central jurisdiction which automatically separated Negro Methodist Churches from white Methodist Churches! Fortunately for all of us this blatant restriction no longer exists and the two segments of our membership are now together!

Jacques Maritain told the truth about all of the churches, both Catholic and Protestant, when he admitted the responsibility of Christians for the atheism of communism. He asked, "What is the cause of this?" and answered, "It is, I hold, because it originated, chiefly through the fault of a Christian world unfaithful to its own principles, in a profound sense of resentment not only against the Christian world, but----and here lies the tragedy-----against Christianity itself." So you recognize the limitations of the position of the Church, of organized Christianity itself. What are you going to put in its place? A fast life; thrills and pleasures; private indulgence? Then do not be too quick to condemn the man who no longer believes in God: For it is perhaps your own coldness and avarice, your own mediocrity and materialism, your own personal sensibility and selfishness that have killed his faith!

A Blessed Confusion

Halford Luccock, a preacher's professor at the Yale Divinity School once told a neighbor of his who had worked himself up to the belief that he was extremely sensitive to noise. He made more noise than anyone else on the block, complaining about the noise the neighbors made. But he never noticed that he had a highly selective attention. H had three children and they made a lot of noise. Dr. Luccock discovered only gradually that what this man wanted above all else was to restore the kingdom of quiet that had prevailed before the children joined the family parade! That couldn't be done! For family life, he said, "Is like universal history. It's divided into two epochs. B. C. and A. D. B. C. meaning "before children," and A. D. meaning after the deluge."

A family with children is not a kingdom of peace. It is a democracy of noise, a blessed confusion." Family life----"A blessed confusion!"

There are families that I've observed where there seems to be plenty of confusion but in no sense the thought that it may be blessed. In some families there is the constant refrain of you can't do that because I said so! In others, the raised hand symbolizing threat, attempted control through the use of force irrespective of any other consideration.

Then there is the family where one or both parents constantly say, "If we only didn't have kids to take care of, how nice life might be!" And they say this continually within the hearing of the children....."If only I didn't have to take care of....., I might be able to do some of these other things....." Is family life viewed as a blessed confusion for these people? I'm afraid not.

On the occasion of the beginning of National Family Week, I should like to share with you some thought concerning family life. You're probably right in asking what do you know about family life? You don't even have one! I'll admit, there was a time before Julie and I had a family in which your criticism would have counted, but since the early sixties we've had a family and understand what is involved in raising one! Nevertheless, we both believe the family is and has been a "blessed confusion."

The first thought that comes to mind on this subject is that a family should be planned. This has been said before, but should be said over and over again. "It's a mistake to think that a family just comes about naturally!" It does in one sense only. You carry out the biological action and children may follow. But to think that we can do nothing about when they should come and how often, this is a mistake. June and I decided the date of birth of our children.....It didn't just happen. It reminds me of a conversation I had with a young mother who said the children just keep coming.....I've been to the doctor but what he says doesn't seem to help. It was only after my third child in three years that I found out my husband was Catholic!

You and I should plan not only for the arrival of our children, but also for their futures....Will we be able to buy them the food and clothes they'll need? Will we be able to have a pleasant home for them? Will we be able to provide them with the opportunities of growth in body and mind so necessary for the wholesome development of their personalities? If not, then we can certainly question how well prepared we are to have a family. Could your family then be the one from whom all families of the earth are blessed?

Secondly, are you sure of your role in the family? There is little so devastating to family life than confusion which results from members of the family having lost the sense of knowing what their role is in the family.....I know of more than one man who feels at a complete loss to know what he and his wife should do in their family life.....They seems to have lost the knowledge or perhaps never had it that they are a loving husband of their wives and the father of their children. I know of one man in particular who has completely lost his knowledge of what his role is in the family. And it's a pathetic state of affairs to be in. He doesn't know how to exercise any authority in his family. He's totally dependent upon his wife to make all of the decisions not only for the whole family, but for himself as well. He's abdicated his role as father and head of the household for a position of complete dependence upon his wife. His children taunt him and make fun of him..... They're as confused as he is to find their father is like a child himself. He's not a man with confidence in himself. He doesn't bring himself to use any discipline upon his children. He fears a loss of their love for him of he tried to act as a father should.....He seems to have forgotten only a man can be a father.....

Take the role a woman plays in family life. Notice how many women are confused by both what their role should be in the family, they're betwixt and between.....Should they work outside of the home and help be the provider or should they stay at home and take care of the house and concern themselves with the needs of their children and husband? What should I do is the question she asks continually. She no longer seems to know what her role is. She seems to have forgotten only a woman can be a mother.

Do you know what your role is in the family? If not, you will be confused without knowing why. Are you satisfied with what you are doing in your present family situation?

Thirdly, have you reminded yourself lately what the purpose of family life really is? One great theological and sociologist has written, "The crisis of modern family life will not be met until men and women intend responsible marriage, adequately prepare for it, and carry it out in good faith. Christian marriage is a permanent partnership in moral development and the joyous sharing of love and companionship between the parents with children who are brought into the family." There is no substitute for family life nor at the same time more difficult an experience than fulfilling the purpose of family life. There is one church whose view of family life is essentially procreative, human reproduction is the chief purpose of men and women in marriage. It's almost like saying we don't care about the quality of life we just want life…..And it's true, isn't it, many people don't stop to think what the purpose of family life may be…..that it's just a matter of having a few kids, a comfortable home, a steady job and as few problems as possible through the course of life. But is this the real purpose of family life? Notice what each of these things is, having a few kids, a comfortable home, a steady job, few problems. Not one of these has anything to do with the quality of life involved! Family life for many is almost as if a man were asked what he wanted more than anything else in the world and he replied, financial security for the rest of his life. We're always on the edge of something. We don't seem to remember the purpose at all of what we do.....We don't even stop to realize what originally brought us together as man and wife.....It's somehow forgotten, pushed aside as impractical and irrelevant to life and we look at the outside of things.....The kind of house we have, the amount of income we'll have, the avoidance of all difficulties and involvements other than what interests us.....

What is the central purpose of family life? You'll laugh when you hear it.....You'll say, that's a preacher for you, always talking about it. Then you'll promptly forget it before you leave this church this morning! You won't even think of it again as you ignore the other people in church this morning. You'll not even begin to think of it as your young son asks you if you'll come out and play with him this afternoon; You'll deny it as you tell your daughter she can't go out with so and so because you don't want her going out with anyone of that nationality. You'll continue to deny it even as you've done ever since you got her to say yes so many years ago! You say it was silly sentimentalism that ever allowed you to believe that family life could be the best way to describe the way you felt about him or her.....but it's still the only purpose for which life was created! Your children won't just evolve into a knowledge of it. No matter how many vitamins, doctors, gadgets, toys, progressive public schools you give them, it still can never compensate for it what is the full-time vocation of the marriage partners. Not even the two income family can buy it.....The way in which we speak of the purpose of family life reminds me of the allegory Hugh Price Hughes wrote concerning "The City of Everywhere."

It is the tale of a man who might have been me, for I dreamed one time of journeying to that metropolis. I arrived early one morning. It was cold. There were snow flurries on the ground and as I stepped from the train to the platform I noticed that the baggageman and the red cap were warmly attired in heavy coats and gloves, but oddly enough, they wore no shoes. My initial impulse was to ask the reason for this odd practice, but repressing it I passed into the station and inquired the way to the hotel. My curiosity, however, was immediately enhanced by the discovery that no one in the station wore any shoes. Boarding the streetcar, I saw that my fellow travelers were likewise barefoot and upon arriving at the hotel, I found the bell hop, the clerk and the habitues of the place were all without shoes.

"Unable to restrain myself any longer, I asked the ingratiating manager what the practice meant."

"What practice?" said he.

"Why, I said pointing to his bare feet. Why don't you wear any shoes in this town? \"

"Ah," he said. "That's just it. Why don't we?"

"But what is the matter? Don't you believe in shoes?"

"Believe in shoes, my friend! I should say we do. That is the first article of our creed, shoes. They are indispensable to the well-being of humanity. Such chilblains, cuts, sores, suffering, as shoes prevent! It's wonderful!"

"Well, then why don't you wear them?" I asked bewildered.

"Ah," said he. "That's just it. Why don't we?"

Though considerably nonplussed, I checked in, secured my room and went directly to the coffee shop and deliberately sat down by an amiable looking gentleman who like wise conformed to the conventions of his fellow citizens. He wore no shoes. Friendly enough, he suggested after we had eaten that we look about the city. The first thing we noticed upon emerging from the hotel was a huge brick structure of impressive proportions. To this building he pointed with pride.

"You see that?" said he. "That is one of our outstanding shoe manufacturing establishments."

"A what?" I asked in amazement. You mean you make shoes there?"

"Well, not exactly," said he, a bit abashed. "We talk about making shoes there and believe me, we've got one of the most brilliant young fellows you have ever heard. He talks most thrillingly and convincingly every week on this great subject of shoes. He has a most persuasive and appealing way. Just yesterday he moved the people profoundly with his exposition of the necessity of shoe-wearing. Many broke down and wept. It was really wonderful!"

"But why don't they wear them?" said I insistently.

"Ah," said he, putting his hand upon my arm and looking wistfully into my eyes,

"That's just it, why don't we?"

Just then, as we turned down a side street, I saw through a cellar window a cobbler actually making a pair of shoes. Excusing myself from my friend I burst into the little shop and asked thee shoemaker how it happened that his shop was not overrun with customers? Said he. "Nobody wants my shoes. They just talk about them."

"Give me what pairs you have already," said I eagerly and paid him thrice the amount he modestly asked. Hurriedly, I returned to my friend and proffered them to him, saying, Here, my friend, some one of these pairs will surely fit you. Take them, put them on. They will save you untold suffering."

But he looked embarrassed, in fact, he was well-nigh overcome with chagrin.

"Ah, thank you," he said, politely, "But you don't understand. It just isn't being done. The front families, well, I….."

"But why don't you wear them?" said I dumbfounded.

"Ah," said he, smiling with his accustomed ingratiating touch of practical wisdom. "That's just it. Why don't we?"

And coming out of the "City of Everywhere" into the Here, over and over and over that query rang in my ears, "Why don't we? Why don't we? Why don't we?

"Why call ye me, Lord, Lord, and do not the things I command you?"

Why aren't we fulfilling the purpose of family life?

An Understanding Mind

The splendor of Solomon was unsurpassed. The might of his kingdom had left an impressive impact upon the nations around Israel. The physical comfort of the king was the object of every subject. The wealth of Solomon was fabulous and even today he is still used as a picture of riches, splendor, power, comfort, and wealth. All of the so-called good things of life. The desires of so many human hearts were Solomon's. He lacked of nothing. His reign as king had just begun and the thing he asked for more than anything else was an understanding mind with which to govern his people.

Think of the things he might have asked for! More wealth, more power, more comfort, more personal pleasure…..Jus a word from the king and thousands would have instantly done his bidding. But Solomon asked for an understanding mind with which to govern his people! Anyone who works with people has this fundamental choice to make-----self-indulgence or self-restraint---privilege or perspective-----thoughtless disregard of others or an understanding mind!

On the occasion of this recognition Sunday, when our church leaders are to be installed for this year of leadership, I should like to share with you some ideas about the qualities necessary for good leadership. For unless we persistently remind ourselves of what constitutes good leadership, we fall into the habit of asking for power while withholding privilege; of exploiting others to further our own ends; of inflating our egos while neglecting our responsibilities.

The first personal quality of good leadership is to have a real concern for people. Unless a person has this quality, he/she is not really fulfilling his/her task fully. He/she will be like the man who moved into a small town in Pennsylvania. On his first day in town he got into a conversation with an old Quaker who was in the habit of sitting on a bench in the quiet square in the center of the little town.

"What kind of people live here?" he asked. The old Quaker replied, "What kind of people didst thee live among before?" "Oh they were mean, narrow, suspicious and very unfair," answered the newcomer. "Then," said the Quaker. "I am sorry, but thee will find the same manner of people here."

They sat in silence for sometime when another newcomer came and asked the same question. The old Quaker asked again, "What manner of people didst thee live amongst before?" A warm smile spread over the newcomer's face. "Friend," he answered, "They were the best folk in the world. They were always friendly, kind, and lovable and I hated to leave them." The old Quaker beamed. "Welcome, neighbor," he said. "Be of good cheer, for thee will find the same people here."

Unless we have a real concern for people we'll never really be able to live with them and understand them. Unless we have a concern for others, then the course of our actions will continually be tested by it.

A girl told me years ago the reason she was no longer interested in her sorority was because of the racial discrimination practiced by it. The case she was referring to was the exclusion of Negroes and Jews from being able to join it. She felt this wasn't fair. She had a real concern for people and this concern automatically kept her from being a part of an unjust discrimination.

This concern for people should lead us to see that the highest values are human values that represent the best of human effort and achievement. Apart from a basic concern for people our leadership would be empty.

The second personal quality necessary for good leadership is an open mind. During youth day at Annual Conference some years ago, Dr. Warren Odom introduced "John Methodist" to us. One of the major features of John Methodist was this: he had an open mind. He was not so much interested in creeds and dogmas as he was in truth and considering all sides of an issue. He did not mistrust honest doubt, but saw within it the way toward greater knowledge and insight into the way God works. He was a person willing to concede that truth without reason was not truth, but wishful thinking. He has his eye upon an unfolding truth as well as realizing a claim on truth as seen in Jesus. He realizes he can be wrong and, therefore, must listen and gather as much information concern ing life as possible while continuing in his beliefs. But these are not held absolutely beyond question, but may themselves render scrutiny.

We've all had the experience of meeting the "closed-mind" within another person. One who acts as if he knew all truth and therefore, anyone who disagrees is obviously mistaken, a person who never quite gets the point that he might be wrong.....I've been privileged to know one or two of these people in my early years. They are sort of like the mother who watched her son parade by with his army unit and she turned to her neighbor and said, "Look at all those foolish boys. They're all out of step, except my Wilbur!" Having an open mind means we can see our own mistakes as well as those that others make and are not afraid to admit it!

The third personal quality of good leadership is an attitude of humility. Isn't it a remarkably radical insight that Jesus said "If any one would be first, he must be last of all and servant of all."

Dr. Leslie Weatherhead, former minister of the famed City Temple in London, England once told his congregation that a distinguished specialist of London had given him two years to live. He remembered seeing his picture in a newspaper and being startled by his own haggard appearance. It was a terrible time for him and he would never forget it. He, quite frankly, did not expect to recover or even to preach again. After months of depression, disappointment, and sadness, he was able to resume that part of this work which consisted in counseling people who had emotional problems. The first person he saw gripped his hand at the end of the session and said, "Thank you. You've helped me very much." From that moment, with the consciousness of being able to help someone else, the tide of his own recovery set in. "He who will find his life must lose it" and "he who will be first must be last of all and servant of all....."

An attitude of humility.....if only we would see ourselves as we really are! James M. Barrie, a noted author, once wrote, "The life of every man is a diary in which he means to write one story, and writes another; and his humblest hour is when he compares the volume as it is with what he vowed to make it. When we look over what we've said and then see what we've done.....When we think back over what we promised and what we actually did, when we review our early hopes and plans and then see what we've actually accomplished how could we be anything but humbled by the contrast!

I read an article in the Reporter Magazine years ago entitled "Our so-called Moral Crisis." The upshot of it was that we have always had people who are going to tell us how washed or how good we have been and that it's rather ridiculous to try to determine how moral or immoral our society is. Where is there an attitude of humility in a report such as this? Must we spell out exactly why it is harmful to cheat.....or lie, or steal, or overindulge in luxury or comfort? Are we so audaciously proud that we cannot even see when and how our values are being undermined? Where is the humility to see when and where we make mistakes? It is everlastingly true that only with a humble and contrite heart can a person see the mistakes he makes?

The fourth and final personal quality necessary for good leadership is to desire to become an example of what we believe.

If we believe that dishonesty is an evil, we must become honest in our relationships with our fellow human beings. If we believe that racial discrimination is inherently unjust and evil, we must overcome our feelings of mistrust and work toward the elimination of racial prejudice within the community and within ourselves. If we believe that alcohol prevents human personality from reaching its highest expression, we must refrain from drinking it ourselves. If we believe that truth and goodness are the ultimate purposes of God's will, we must speak truthfully and practice goodness throughout our lifetimes.

If we believe that love is the highest expression of God's nature, we must love one another without exception. If we believe that Jesus represents the clearest example of God's truth, goodness, and love can we possibly do anything less than follow his example in our personal lives and social relationships? There is no finer testimony to what you believe than by the life that you live.

The story is told of a missionary in China years ago who travelled through an out of the way Chinese town. He found a crowd gathering around him and he told them the story of Jesus. He noticed that the people were exceptionally interested and attentive. When finished the head man said, "Yes, we know him. He used to live here." The missionary tried to explain that he had been talking of one who lived in another century and in another country. They then took him to the cemetery and showed him the grave of an English medical missionary, who a few years before had served healed persons and then died there. They had known him and knowing him meant they had also known the one whose servant he was.

Good leadership requires a concern for people, an open-mind, an attitude of humility and a desire to become what we believe.....

"Give thy servants, oh God, understanding minds with which to govern thy people." Help them to lead us into an appreciation of the service each of us may render to one another and of the example we may become of thy truth, goodness, and love.

Chance Favors The Trained Mind

Ralph W. Sockman once told the story of how Louis Pasteur discovered the principle of vaccination. His discovery came about through the error of an assistant in his laboratory who failed to feed certain cultures properly. When Pasteur was taunted by his critics who said that he had stumbled on his discovery by chance, he replied simply, "True, but chance favors the trained mind."

"Chance favors the trained mind" because the trained mind narrows the area of the unknown. It recognizes certain cues that turn up. It knows how to use the opportunities that arise.

At one of the Palm Sunday breakfasts that we had in East Syracuse sixty years ago. a few of us were talking about a young woman who had just a few days earlier struck a high tension utility pole and proceeded to get out of her car and was immediately electrocuted because her leg had touched the metal strip on the edge of the car as she got out. The man across the table from us said she probably should have stayed in her car until someone came by who knew something about electricity or who could at least have told her how to get out. She didn't know and neither did she know anything about it and subsequently was killed as much by her ignorance as by the electricity. And then this man went on to say (he was a retired industrial arts teacher)that most people know little or nothing about electricity and probably it's just as well they know only that it's dangerous. But it's the safest and most helpful thing in the world if you know how to use it. I couldn't help but think, how tragically true it had been for the young expectant mother who knew nothing about electricity that chance favors the trained mind and may destroy the untrained one......

Have you ever gotten into a discussion with a person who says "Trust yourself and no one else!"

Now on a first hearing you might think this is pretty good advice. Sure it's a good idea to trust yourself, but you'd also better be sure that there's nothing else that you need to learn; that you've got all the answers to all of life's problems and questions; that you can recognize all of the cues that chance may have in store for you!

Probably the hardest person to convince about the need for continual training is one who's mind is already made up. I stopped long ago trying to live our peoples' lives...... And whenever a parent called about his or her daughter or son years ago when I was a practicing Minister and they wanted me to talk him out of getting married or dropping out of school or going somewhere on a trip, the first things I suggested was that the parents come in to talk about it. Because obviously this was a decision they needed to learn to accept no matter how hard it may be for them. All we could try to do was provide the surroundings, the opportunities, the conditions wherein the child discovers the fact that chance favors the trained mind, far more than the untrained one......And when you hear as I heard one evening "What's the use of killing yourself by studying all the time and why spend all this time studying and why spend all this time that you will never use. I can't see that!" You realize with an aching heart he had not yet learned the truth of what you've discovered and what Pasteur said "Chance favors the trained mind!"

On May 24, 1738 a young man attended a worship service in Aldersgate Street Chapel. A man was reading Martin Luther's preface to the Epistle to the Romans. At about a quarter to nine, while this man was reading Luther's description of the change which God works in the heart through faith in Christ this young man felt his heart strangely warmed. Of course you know who this young man was.....It was John Wesley and with the chance coincidence of the needs of this person, at that time and place, with the richness of his long years of studied preparation, John Wesley was able to pick up the cues which transformed his life and enabled him to remold the religious life of England.

On the occasion of Aldersgate Sunday, as it's called in the Methodist Church, I should like to have us examine the meaning, the occurrence, and the implications of this word chance which seems to play such a large part in the thinking of persons who believe all they need is a chance. a stroke of good fortune and all of their problems will be solved.

Consider first of all the meaning of chance. Webster's New World Dictionary defines it as a happening; a fortuitous event; an accidental circumstance; In other words, it's something that can't be counted on. It cannot be assumed that it will ever happen or occur. How do you usually take a trip? Just start out in no particular direction or purpose in mind? Or do we at least know where you want to be at a certain time? I can just imagine what some of you are thinking.....What do you want us to do? Work as hard on our vacation as we do during the rest of the year? We're not interested in a planned trip. We want to relax and enjoy ourselves. In one sense I can appreciate your feelings on this somewhat. You want an element of chance to operate in your travel agenda. Discover your own delightful little restaurants and motels along the way.

A couple who are very good friends of ours travel to Illinois each year from New England to visit his parents. The wife plans the trip months in advance. She contacts the Automobile Club and has them plot the best route for them to take. She writes ahead to the Chamber of Commerce in several states to get brochures and all the information she can get about what's especially historical or beautiful along their route to see as they're passing through. She doesn't want to miss anything. Her husband told us that after the first trip to Illinois and back, his wife knew all of the best motels to stay in, she knew where all of the Atlantic Service Stations were (in which to use their credit card) and how often to stop in order to use the rest rooms! She wanted to be as thoroughly prepared as possible. I'm not suggesting that it's necessary to be completely prepared to remove all elements of chance as that. But, because chance is an accidental circumstance, you can't plan on finding a motel vacant after a long day's drive, or an appetizing restaurant just anywhere, or even a gas station with a clean and serviceable rest room for that matter. If you've done any long distance traveling, you know what an accidental circumstance it is to find these kinds of facilities.

Chance means a happening---a fortuitous event---an accidental circumstance. It's not something you can plan on. That's why you have to use the soundest judgment that you can, because chance is an event outside the realm of our expectation. I've met any number of people who were traveling around the world in the midst of the ancient scenes and ruins in the art to history and never seemed to have any idea or knowledge of their significance. They were just taking their chances that they might learn something enroute. Probably the best illustration of this was the man returning with his wife from a two year stay in the Philippines where he had been a sales representative for Caterpillar Construction Equipment Company. We had just heard a guide describe the history of the construction of the Parthenon on the Acropolis in Athens, Greece and how it had stood until the seventeenth century when the roof was accidentally blown off in a war between the Austrians and the Turks. As we were walking through the huge columns of the Parthenon, he looked up at the open roof and said, "This will really be a wonderful building when they finish rebuilding it!" I'll never forget the look on the face of the man who was a retired Professor of History when he heard this man's words. He was taking his chances in getting a bit of Art Culture and History never realizing the importance of what he saw as a priceless piece of antiquity which could never be duplicated again…..Chance, then, means because it is an accidental circumstance we cannot simply drive along waiting for it to happen!

Secondly, consider its occurrence. Chance is so rare, so haphazard that it is not a generally recognized unit, long after it has happened. I suppose the only place where this recognition of chance isn't long after the event, but soon after, is a game of cards. Have you ever noticed how the husband says to his wife, why in the world didn't you play your ace on that last trick? It would have been the best chance to catch all those counters! And so for the rest of the night and the next few weeks he's apt to keep bringing up the fact that she missed her one big chance to win the game! But aside from playing cards or chess or some other game, chance makes a rare occurrence in the life of man. Certainly not where it's recognized as an event that held incalculable consequence for history in a few brief days, hours, or minutes. One of these moments of chance that occurred in World War II was at the battle of El-Alamain. Just before the battle the Germans had run out of fresh drinking water and had come upon a pipe of water left by the retreating British forces. Unknown to the Germans, the British had deliberately extended the pipe line out into the Mediterranean Sea before their retreat and the thirsty Germans, thinking it was fresh water, drank heavily of this salt water since their own supply had been exhausted. Shortly thereafter the British troops attacked and after hours of fierce fighting, the throat-parched Germans and Italians best a hasty retreat back across the dessert as much from thirst as from the attacking British Eighth Army!

Historians are known for their discovery of the rare occurrence of chance in battles or human affairs which, if it had not occurred, might have spelled an entirely different outcome on the course of history. In the early sixties a book was written entitled "The Guns of August". It showed how the fate of World War I was sealed in the first month of the war with the battle of the Marne River finally deciding the stalemating effect of trench warfare for the next four years!

Shortly after this book was published, another book came out entitled "Dare Call It Treason" where the author pointed out that by June of 1917 out of some 100 infantry divisions, the French High Command could count on the fighting obedience of only two of these divisions. The German generals had heard of the rank mutinies of the French forces, but they could not believe that such rebellions could occur, even among Frenchmen. Thus, by the time they did attack in July 1917 they ran into the reconditioned forces of Field Marshal Petain who had done so much to rebuild the moral of French troops and were stopped after some initial success.

Chance rarely occurs and is not always recognized until long after the influence of its occurrence has passed.

Finally, in light of the meaning and occurrence of chance, consider your life. There are certain elements of chance inherent in the origin of our lives that certain chance facts came together giving us the body structure, the color eyes and hair, the texture of our skin, the mental ability and motor ability that we have, all the products of chance combinations of the genes of our parents. Likewise, there's a certain indefiniteness about our futures even as there has been in the past. A great number of unknowns stand before us and yet we cannot count on chance. We know it may be a part of our future, but we cannot count on it. We cannot use chance as an excuse for real effort on our part. We have to be prepared for the utilization of chance, to turn it into an opportunity or an advantage when and if it comes. We have to be ready to turn chance into an advantage even though it may not appear to be an advantage at first.

I suppose this is why Protestant churches stand pretty firmly united against betting, bingo and gambling of any sort…..because we believe it detracts from humans' initiative and activity so that we forget that life requires work, effort, striving, growing through our lifetimes. We cannot rest and wait for chance to accomplish what we did not attempt to do or create.

There's a song that used to be pretty popular years ago: "Que sera, sera, Whatever will be, will be." Now if that isn't a type of fatalistic giving up of human activity, I don't know what is! It's a new and modern form of a very old and ancient pessimism…..Giving up! What's the use! There's no sense to human life, there's no purpose to it so why do anything about it?

Whenever I hear a person talk like this I feel like saying "Then at least be ready to die- Prepare yourself for death and get out of this silly idea that there's nothing more to do in life! While we're on the subject of death, incidentally, let me remind you of how necessary this preparation is for your children as well as for yourselves. Use the chance occurrence of the death of a pet, a bird, a tree as an opportunity for your child to grow in his/her understanding that one day every living thing must die. There is a return of living creatures to the soil. It is part of the normal sequence of events for living things. It prepares the way for the child to accept death as an expected part of life even as the memory of that former living creature continues on with him/her for a lifetime. Without some advance preparation of this sort the death of a member of the family may become an emotional block in the child's life which will continue throughout his/her lifetime to haunt him/her with a fear and dread of death.

Consider the implication for your life in the words of Louis Pasteur that "Chance favors the trained mind."

The story is told of the late Sir Alexander Fleming that as a boy he wished desperately to become a doctor. He went as far as he could in his studies in the village school of Lochfield, Scotland but upon graduating with big honors from high school, his father told him he couldn't afford to send him to the medical school. Young Alexander Fleming was heartbroken because he had his heart set upon becoming a doctor. It was all part of a sad summer day for him as he got a job as a local apprentice when on his way home one evening he heard a young boy crying for help where he had fallen into the village pond. Alexander Fleming plunged in clothes and all and hauled the frightened boy out safe and sound on shore and then went on his way home. When the boy's father found out what had happened he went to the Fleming home and said he should like to repay the young man in some way for saving his son from drowning. The elder Fleming said his son had his heart set on becoming a doctor but that he had no money with which to send him. The grateful father of the rescued boy said he would be glad to see that he got his medical education and paid for all of the studies of Alexander Fleming which he would have. For Mr.Churchill was so grateful that young Alexander Fleming had saved his son Winston Churchill from drowning. And a young man who has prepared himself well for this opportunity and another who prepared himself to save his country each in his own way stands as a tremendous illustration of the fact that "Chance favor the trained mind!"

A Modern Instance

Outside of Cairo in a place called Sapphora, workman were busy clearing the sand away from the broken and buried statue of Ramses II. He was once one of the mightiest and greatest of the Pharaohs and leader of a mighty nation and empire. An empire that boasted some of the greatest works of art in the history of humankind. And yet mighty Ramses and his Egyptian Empire both are part of the dust and colossal debris of history.

When I first saw the scene I could not help but recall the words of the poet Shelley who wrote of another ancient king: "My hame is Ozymandias, King of Kings: Look on my works, ye Mighty and despair!" Nothing beside me remains. Round the decay of that colossal wreck, boundless and bare, the lone and level sands stretch far away!

To hear our two presidential candidates of the early sixties speak, you would think the greatness of America lies in her military strength and the naked power of gigantic force. To hear Mr. Kruschov speak during the early sixties you would have thought the Soviet Union was the world's hope because of her vast armies and ponderous array of missiles and hydrogen bombs.

It was Adolf Hitler who said in a special message to his troops in the pre-dawn of September 1, 1939 touching off World War II with the invasion of Poland "The course upon which you are embarking today will secure the future of the Third Reich for a thousand years!"

It has been thus for more than five thousand years that men have sought to affirm their faith in the instruments of power and might, and yet "nothing beside remains. Round the decay of that colossal wreck, boundless and bare, than lone and level sands stretch far away!"

The facts of history affirm that each successive empire has been or is swept away. The Egyptian, the Assyrian, the Babylonian, the Persian, the Greek, the Roman, the Byzantine, the Holy Roman, the Portuguese, the Spanish, the Dutch, the Chinese, the German, the Russian, the Japanese, The French and the British empires have all but disappeared.

It was Ezekiel who saw how this process worked in his time even as it still works with us today. "And all the trees of the field shall know that I the Lord bring low the high trees and make high the low tree, dry up the green tree, and make the dry tree flourish." Later it was Jesus who said "And every one who exalteth himself shall be abased and he that humbleth himself shall be exalted."

The main fact of history is this that the powerful are made low and the low are made high. When William Dean Howells first used the title "A Modern Instance" for one of his books, he wished to portray the recurrence of an old old problem of human life. And this was more that one hundred years ago. It was a modern instance then and still is and will continue to be so long as unlimited pride is a part of human experience. It was Reinhold

Niebuhr who wrote "The whole history of racial, national, religious and other social struggles is a commentary on the objective wickedness and social miseries which result from self-righteousness."

Pride, be it national or personal, public or private leads to the downfall of nations and of men. "Nothing beside remains. Round the decay of that colossal wreck, boundless and bare, the lone and level sands stretch far away."

There are three cautions I would suggest we keep in mind as we view the course of our lives. We have a habit of overlooking the dangers of pride especially when we see it so blatantly manifested in the international arms races, military parades, or personal smugness of political leaders.

The first mistake we must avoid is believing might makes right! Augustine gave an excellent example of how easy it is to believe where power is there is justice also! He told of a Mediterrean pirate caught by Alexander the Great of Greece who asked him, "How dare you molest the seas so? The pirate replied with a free spirit, How dare you molest the whole world? Because I do it with a little ship only I am called a thief; but you doing it with a great navy are called a conquerer!"

That's just it.....because a nation or a person is powerful or had a great deal of influence or exercises strong economic control, this is no reason to assume they are therefore always right! During the 19th century successive English patriots and poets proclaimed "We live or die for England, right or wrong!" This attitude may have been accepted then, indeed was demanded of all who were considered worthy English sons, but this attitude is lethal today. This is exactly what we found so exasperating among the Nazis after World War II, the plea for each person up for war comes trial was "they were simply following orders."

Might does not make right. Remember how it was as children? There was the school yard bully who always made it hard for us. He threatened and we'd do just about anything he wanted. Imagine how it would have been if we hadn't recourse to a higher justice from our teachers than the will of might imposed by the school-yard bully! And yet in subtle ways we still dispense justice on the school boy level. We give foreign aid only to countries who will be our allies or from whom we obtain special privileges of trade, resources or bases. We encourage graft and corruption in local government by keeping people in office for years without demanding an accounting of their views and proposals concerning the issues. We practice religious intolerance when we feel we are threatened by an increasing practice of religious intolerance when we feel we are threatened by an increasing preponderance of those who hold different beliefs. We accept dishonesty on the part of businessmen who pad expense accounts as legitimate expenses acquired by business necessity. We jail income tax evaders, criminals, prostitutes, alcoholics, but those who extort money from small business operators for protection against possible harm, what is done about them? The protection racket is one of the most serious crimes perpetuated in America today and little or nothing is being done about it. We still labor under the illusion that might makes right!

What match was the manager in Bethlehem for the palace in Rome? Where, but in Rome, is there ancient might and splendor? "Nothing beside remains. Round the decay of that colossal wreck, boundless and bare, the lone and level sands stretch far away."

Our second caution is we must not mistake the obvious for the truth. It was quire obvious that the splendor of Rome outshone the shabby, dingy little cow barn in Bethlehem. It was quite obvious that the armed chariots and soldiers of the Pharaoh were more than a match for the motley thousands of Israeli slaves in bondage in Egypt. I was obvious that the followers of Jesus and Paul were few in number while the Roman Empire was of vast size. It was obvious that the British Empire was the greatest in the history of mankind and the thirteen American colonies were simply primitive wilderness outposts on the rim of this empire. It was obvious the papacy was the strongest power on the European continent and Martin Luther was just a rebellious nuisance. It was obvious the Czarist police were the most ruthless, cruel and powerful the Russian Empire had ever known and the communists were weak and few in number. It was obvious the British government of India had supreme authority over the Indian people and Gandhi was just a little man with a few followers. It was obvious Chiang Kai-Shek ruled China at the end of World War II and Mao-Tsetung was contained within the mountain fastness of Yenan with a few thousand communist troops.

It was obvious that a boat couldn't be powered by steam and that Robert Fulton was a fool. It was obvious that Alaska was nothing more than an icebox and seven million, two hundred thousand dollars was a waste of good tax payers' money. It was obvious that man wasn't made to fly. The Wright Brothers were lunatics to think man could fly.

The confirmation of history is that what is most obvious is not necessarily the truth. The pharisee thought himself to be better than the publican. He felt himself justified before God for all that he did. And yet his obvious goodness was not the true spirit of humility so necessary for the growth of human understanding. Truth is apt to be the very thing we have overlooked; in the seemingly unimportant and insignificant features of every day life; how we answer questions children ask; how we review our own thoughts and actions; how we talk with one another; how often we stop what we have been doing for a long time and ask why am I doing this? Unless we continually review and rethink what we've taken for granted we may be like the man of whom Cicero spoke who, as a prisoner, had spent his entire life in a dark dungeon and knew the light of day only from a single beam which filtered through a crack in the prison wall. He was full of woe and distress when he was told that the wall was to be pulled down. "It will rob me of my gleam of light," he said. Not knowing that the destruction of the wall would bathe him in the splendor of daylight and show him the infinite opportunity of the outer world! That which is most obvious is not necessarily the truth.

Third, each nation and each man must seek to do that which is for the international good of human kind. I realize this is a very abstract ideal to try to understand. There are some people who just bristle whenever they hear the word international. There are some people who resent even considering doing something that would help any other person to say nothing of perhaps helping our enemies. Standing in the rain the other morning outside of the gates at General Electric, I couldn't help but see again the need for a lot of work being done along the lines of civic responsibility on the part of both labor and management; that both must learn to exercise the principle of the public good which supersedes their own self-interest. The fate of the world depends on the outcome of this strike! If there is violence and disorder, it will be that much harder to gain respect and mutual appreciation for the other fellow's point of view. If there is a mutually satisfying contract worked out then labor-management relations will improve. In so far as this mutual respect and recognition of the other side's point of view is accepted or rejected to that extent the cause of the world is advanced or hindered by this present impasse at General Electric. Wherever there is a hardening of the artery of self-interest all of us lose; we all suffer. Just look what would happen if we didn't pay taxes! We would be without the benefit of schools, roads, water, sewage and fire protection, police, social security to say nothing of the national benefits derived from our nation's tax revenues. I think we all recognize the futility of the argument that we shouldn't have to pay taxes, but taxation is not evil, it can advance the common good of all of us.

The Philips translation of the Epistle of James puts it right on the line of how important it is what each one does. "But what about the feuds and struggles that exist among you. Where do you suppose they come from? Can't you see that they arise from conflicting passions within yourselves?" And how do wars get started? Because each one of us is a contributor to war because of the personal conflicts in which he engages. You say you do not like your neighbor next door? You say your boss insulted you?

You say your wife will have to apologize to you for losing her temper? You say you aren't going to visit your aunt again until she learns she can't tell you what to do? You say you're going to force your child to obey you if its the last thing you ever do? You say you'll never forgive your husband for going out with that woman?

Is it any wonder that nations cannot get along with other nations and that wars get started? What happens to each of us happens to the nations and ultimately to the world! "God, be merciful to me a sinner!"

The Reflected Spirit

King Solomon once summoned two skilled craftsmen and ordered each to build a room of unequaled magnificence. They could request any material no matter how costly, and it would be given to them. The king warned, however: "At the end of six months, the work must be completed! I personally will examine the results of your labors." If their efforts met with his approval. there would be a generous reward; if not, the penalty would be death.

One of the workmen was diligent and began at once to requisition costly materials, precious jewels and delicately woven fabrics. Th either workman was lazy and assured himself he had sufficient time and need not exert himself unduly.

Two months passed and the industrious workman had made considerable progress in building his room. But the lazy workman had not even started. By the end of the fifth month the work of the former was nearing completion. He now had an additional month to perfect the room to his satisfaction. The lazy workman, who had not even started, now realized he had but one month to work. Dismay and panic seized him as he remembered Solomon's warning. Looking at the nearly completed room of this fellow workman, he was awed by its workmanship and indescribable beauty. What could he do? He gave himself up for lost until he conceived of a plan to deceive Solomon, save his life, and set the same time merit a generous reward.

Since his room was to be adjacent to the room of the diligent artisan, he requisitioned nothing but mirrors. With the mirrors carefully placed on the walls and ceiling, his room reflected the magnificence of the adjoining room. A quick glance would reveal two identical rooms. Satisfied that his hoax would be effective, he confidently awaited the inspection of the king. Shortly thereafter, Solomon came to view the results. He first entered the room of the diligent workman and was enthralled with its magnificence. Then he turned to the work of the lazy artisan and was amazed to behold a room of equal beauty and magnificence. Nodding to both workmen, he summoned them to appear at the palace to receive their reward.

Considerably relieved, the lazy workman gloated at having so easily deceived the wise Solomon. Grateful that God had granted him the health and the skill to complete his work, the diligent workman breathed a silent prayer of gratitude. At the palace the king ordered his servants to place a large bag of gold upon the table, and to the industrious workman he announced, "This is your reward." The latter gratefully accepted the gold and returned to his family.

The lazy workman struggled to conceal his satisfaction as Solomon had another large bag of gold placed upon the table. As the artisan stepped forward to claim his reward, the king commanded, "Wait!" The startled workman stopped as Solomon placed a mirror next to the bag of gold. Pointing to the reflection in the mirror Solomon turned to the workman and said, "The reflection is your reward!"

This workman failed to realize that whatever it is we do it is but a reflection of the spirit within us! If we are diligent, honest, trustworthy, then the work of our hands will but reflect this inner spirit within us. If we are careless, scheming, and dishonest, this too will be reflected in all that we do!

The 20th century has been called "the century of the common man." Indeed, the harvest of rights and privileges which we have obtained today are but the fruits of nine thousand years of human sacrifice and suffering. We have come to take them altogether too lightly and easily.

This is labor day weekend and once again we would commemorate and think upon the theme found in the letter of James as he wrote "What does it profit, my brethren, if a man says he has faith, but has not works? Can his faith save him? So faith by itself, if it has no works, is dead." 'Show me your faith apart from your works, and I, by my works, will show you my faith.'

There is no separation between how and what we think and what we do. Peter, as he was in the very act of denying that he knew Jesus, was betrayed by his speech. He had the same Galilean accent as did Jesus. And Peter thought he could get out of the responsibility of having to admit he knew him.

And likewise we seem to think we can avoid the reflection of ourselves cast in what we do!

How we do our daily tasks, how well or how poorly we do our jobs, how hard or how little we work is seen as but "the reflected spirit" of what we are!

"Show me your faith apart from your works, and I, by my works, will show you my faith."

On this labor day weekend, when it is well for us to consider and commemorate the rights, privileges, and responsibilities of not only those who work for others, but for all of us for we are all engaged in the universal task of living. We of the 20th century are the harvesters of fruits which have painfully grown for more than nine thousand years of recorded human history involving the untold suffering and sacrifice of billions of people who labored in the undreamed of hope that one day men would reap the rewards of this greatest efforts. This is the only redeeming quality of life, that we live in such a way that we reflect all that is good and noble in humankind for those brief moments of time we have to contribute of ourselves to eternity.

"Show me your faith apart from your works, and I, by my works, will show you my faith." In order to relate ourselves more closely to the ennobling spirit whose reflection we should cast in the workaday world, there are three discoveries which need to be made.

First, we need to discover the meaning of work. We have heard a variety of interpretations given to work, undoubtedly. Some believe it is necessary in order to make a living and it does do that. Some believe it is simply an unpleasant interlude between periods of play or self-indulgence, and we have certainly seen enough examples of that. Some believe it's a necessary evil begotten as a result of Adam and Eve's disobedience in the garden of Eden. Some believe it's a means toward acquiring greater material wealth and comfort. Some believe it's a personal trial testing patience, fortitude, and personal responsibility that must be accepted as a duty of life. All of these beliefs concerning work actually have some merit to them. But are these really the most important meanings of work?

The injunction of Jesus seemed to be that all that we do should represent a prior commitment to God out of which comes the reason for existence: "Seek first the kingdom of God and his righteousness and all these other things shall be added unto you." In other words, work is a part of the way in which we give thanks for life.

Dr. Walter Meulder, Dean of the Seminary at Boston University has written, "Man does not exist for work, but work exists for man, and man exists for God. Man is God's steward as the earth is subdued and cared for. Man's work is thus included within the purpose of God." Another biblical scholar, Bienert out it this way, "Man is to serve God; work serves man and man serves God with and through his work."

"Show me your faith apart from your works, and I, by my works, will show you my faith." This is our faith that each activity is a reflection of the spirit that made us. Is our view of the job we have, of the work we undertake, a reflection of the spirit of God in all that we do? Do we see the meaning of work as an opportunity not only through which we gain a greater personal satisfaction, but also as an opportunity to show our gratitude to God for his gift of life to us?

Our second discovery is that what we do is more than a job. It is a lifetime investment! We hear much of the amount of time which work absorbs and the responses which we some times hear "Wouldn't it be wonderful if we didn't have to work so much or so hard." Yet every activity we carry out is an opportunity of giving witness to the fact that we are investing ourselves inactivities representative of the Spirit which resides in us. The measure of a man is seen in what he does. This is called the principle of performance; we can see how well or how poorly a person does on a job as they give witness to their training and ability in the actual situation.

I've often wondered if a poorly kept house, yard, equipment or children may not be a reflection of our inner confused spirit of those whose responsibility they are? I can recall my mother was insistent that I change from my patched or torn clothes that I might have worn on the farm to better ones when we went shopping or into the city. She recognized the obvious reflection upon her if I should be seen looking more like a tramp than as her son! She cared about the investment she was making in our lives with hers. Our job or our work should be an investment of our lives for the improvement of life around us. Likewise, our external neglect represents our internal lack. One of the symptoms of mental illness is neglect of appearance and reality about us, as if to say symbolically what cannot be said actually. "I don't care about myself or the world because no one cares about me!"

What we do reflects the spirit within us. "Show me your faith apart from your works, and I, by my works, will show you my faith."

Our third discovery to be made is that of appreciation for what each one can contribute to the good of all. Working for a big company or concern is apt to make each person feel pretty small and almost anonymous in the entire mass. But it is exactly at this point that the greatest influence needs to be exercised to offset the lethal affects of this reflection.

We have heard a great deal about the overwhelming and stifling affects of communist collectivism which seemed to quell individual incentives and enterprises. Yet one of the biggest surprises to a group of us sixty years ago was the extent to which the communist government at that time was attempting to arouse their workers of individual pride of work and accomplishment in their workers. Extensive educational programs for the workers were designed to give them a new lease on individual dignity and importance in national projects. Every factory, school, and farm had a super abundance of slogans and charts used as mass appeals to individuals to exert their greatest efforts in order to bring about the great say of world communism! There were individual incentive boosters of higher pay for more work! And the further rather sobering surprise was that it was working! It came as rather a jolt to hear with what naiveté the Russian workmen spoke of their own personal part played in this great world-wide purpose of improving the standard of living for all humankind! Many of the workmen would actually say they would rather like to have a new home, but they would wait until more construction materials would be available to the Chinese or Burmese who needed them so much more desperately. It is this massed affect of millions of individual sacrifices which is gaining for the Russians such large strides in economic power so that they are slowly gaining on our still greater but challenging economic system.

The individual in our way of life must be appreciated and encouraged to realize his own contribution is virtually necessary to the survival of our freer way of life. Individually, this will spell the difference between the success or failure of that way of life. If our faith is empty of good works, woe be our faith. If we neglect the necessity of individual appreciation and willingness to sacrifice for the sake of each other woe be our way of life! We cannot hope to continue to reap the fruits of others if we are not busy planting for posterity. The future of not only our nation and society, but of our families depend upon the reflected spirit witnessed by how we work, what we say. and all that we do! Show me your faith by your works and I, by my works, will show you my faith."

When Opportunity Knocks

Picture if you will the scene, Lot and Abraham standing on the top of a Palestine mountain surveying the land before them. There had been a great deal of controversy between them and each recognized that a parting of the ways was bound to come. And the noble Abraham in a gesture of generosity and kindness said to Lot, "Choose whatever land you want and I'll take what's left." Lot looked over the hills and valleys, deserts and plains and saw the the land along the Jordan river was the best. It was fertile and well watered. The grass and trees grew abundant beside it. And Lot, who had been given the opportunity to choose what he wanted, chose what he thought was the best. He chose the Jordan Valley.

Most preachers stop here and begin to castigate Lot for his greediness and well they should. But what happened to Abraham? Did he simply shrug his shoulders and pass off the incident lightly? I doubt it very much. Abraham probably felt the loss as keenly as any of us might. He was probably discouraged and angered by the turn of events. He had to reorient himself to this loss even as you and I. But amidst the discouragement and despair came the recognition to Abraham even as it desperately needed to come to us "Lift up your eyes, and look from the place where you are!"

From the loss you've suffered at the hands of a greedy and selfish man; from the suffering and heartache left by the death of the one around whose whole life yours had been centered; from the disappointment of failing in a business venture; from the failure of getting into the school you wanted or job you felt you had to have.

"Lift up your eyes, and look from the place where you are!"

No matter whether we have experienced disappointment yet or not, it shall inevitably be upon us. And we too need to see that as one disappointment comes along another opportunity knocks.

Dr. Howard Thurman, one of America's foremost preachers in his day and Dean of the Boston University Chapel wrote, "All around us worlds are dying and new worlds are being born; all around us life is dying and life is being born. The fruit ripens on the tree, the roots are silently at work in the darkness of the earth against a time when there shall be new leaves, fresh blossoms, green fruit. Such is the growing edge! Look well to the growing edge!"

Look well to the opportunities which lie hidden in the most difficult and trying periods of our existence. "Lift up your eyes from the place where you are." What do we need to remember as disappointment, disillusionment, despair, or disaster falls upon us? How may we meet the inevitable calamity to which we are heirs?

First, we need to remember that crisis is a test of our capacity to grow. We've heard much of late from psychologists stating the harm which is unwittingly done by parents when they do not allow their children to learn to make decisions and to accept the consequences of making them. Just last winter I was called upon by one of the foremost dentists of New England to come to spend the night in his home because he was afraid of his thirty eight year old son. His son was breaking furniture, windows, lamps and his father thought he was next. The son has never been allowed to make his own decisions and take the consequences of them. His father was a great man in dentistry and his son was pushed into dentistry; the father was a man of wealth and the son was always provided for and subsidized by his father. The father had a great reputation in dentistry and he would not allow his son to care for his own patients. The father always had the last word. The son had become so dependent upon his father he could not make his own decisions. When he was faintly on his own he made fantastic decisions whose consequences he could not grasp. When I first saw him he was again trying to get money from his father and this time his father refused on the grounds of ill health and age. The son had a little child's temper tantrum but with grown up effects!

Through the meeting of small crises we gain confidence, knowledge and experience fundamentally needed to meet larger ones later. Without them, we do not grow! The comment of our olympic high jump star is a classic in meeting the crisis of defeat after being bent with an attitude which will lead to growth from the experience. "I don't have any alibis. I was beaten fair and square."

Crisis can lead to growth. Is this not the affirmation of the cross? That there is to be no fear in facing the worst that the world can do? The ultimate of pain and agony may lead to growth of spirit undreamed of before the crisis was endured. And Jesus said to his disciples when they were hesitant, despondent and fearful of their mission. "Life up your eyes and see how the fields are already ripe for

harvest." Lift up your eyes from the place where you are."
Without pain there is no growth.

Second, for every challenge, a response must be
made. We make a mistake when we think we need not
act upon a problem or situation facing us. It is told of a
former Senator from Ohio that he knew how to choose
the misty importance of his letters to answer. His
system of correspondence fell into three categories: 1)
information seeking where a constituent wished to have
certain information about the government's bills before
the Senate voted. His secretary took care of this without
even consulting him; 2) The important questioning of
the Senator's views concerning how he will vote. These
he separated according to the rank of the questioner in
state politics. These he would eventually dictate. 3) The
criticisms of his constituents dissatisfied with his voting
record or views in the Senate. These issues required
immediate replies. These letters he kept sometimes carrying
them about for weeks on end, but never answering them.
Perhaps this was the reason why he was not returned to
office several years ago. He had not responded to the
challenge presented to him by dissatisfied constituents.

Where would man be today if it were not for early
man's response to the challenges presented to him? The
overflowing Nile during August and september spread the
wild barley growing along its banks over broader fields
and challenged the early Egyptians to go further in their
search for the barley. Later, the challenge of keeping the
soil moist so that the seed would grow at other times of the
year, brought the response of irrigation. This challenge of
more food brought the response of more people and thus
more villages. Cultivation of land brought the response of
fences and boundaries to keep animals out of crops, thus

learning to the challenge of property and the response of law. As agriculture developed, further challenges presented themselves. New implements and tools were the challenge and small industries were the response to the challenges life presented to him. And today no, differently from the past, new challenges are constantly set before us calling forth new responses which will reflect the continuing process at work in our lives. We are continually called upon to "Lift up our eyes, and look from the place where we are."

Several years ago at the death of his father a friend of mine was inconsolable with grief. He couldn't believe it had happened to him. "Why? Why did it happen to my Dad?" He kept asking himself. He could not understand why, even as all of us fail to understand when it happens. For several days he neither slept not ate very much. He could not talk about his father without breaking down and asking over and over again, Why? Why" Until a few weeks later after the pain and grief had subsided he was once again able to "Life up his eyes and look from the place where he was." Life once again was a challenge to him awaiting his response.

Third, you always have to start where you are! Have you noticed how often people try to start from wishing something were true? They wish they had a bigger house. "If I had a bigger house the rooms wouldn't look so cluttered up.....It reminds me of a woman I know who has so much...."stuff" in each of the rooms of her house you can hardly read a newspaper under one of her many lamps because the light is blocked by the shade of so much stuff! Or others who wish they had more influence in government......They'd see to it that good laws are passed and they haven't voted in years! Or others who wish they had more money, then they could really provide for their families; buy them good food and new clothes…And then they put themselves in debt years on end buying a television set, kitchen appliances or a new car!

A poet of sorts summarized this fruitless business of wishing very cleverly when he wrote, "It's not what you'd do with a million, if riches should ere by your lot, but what are you doing at present with the dollar and a quarter you've got?"

We have to start where we are not where we wish we were! Abraham could have spent all of this time moaning about how Lot had cheated him. He might even have been justified in doing this despite the fact he gave lot his choice. But the revelation which came to Abraham needs to come to us…..We can curse, stamp our feet, become highly indignant or give way to self-pity, but we still have to begin with ourselves!

Advantages can be piled before us for the rest of our lives…..and are…..but we still have to know what to do with them! Opportunities of health, a fulfilling family life, a satisfying job, a loving wife or husband, a comfortable home where each person is interested in the life of the other, good friends with whom we can share our joys as well as your sorrows, our dreams as well as our disappointments, school where we can grow in our awareness of what life is like…..These are but a few of the daily advantages we take for granted…..

"Abraham, life up your eyes and look from the place where you are!" When opportunity knocks, how ready are you to receive it?

Before You Go.....

"What did you expect? Did you really believe he would act differently? If you take a man out of his home environment where he is surrounded by members of his family, friends, and all the people who have become a part of his world, he'll not act the same. He'll do things that he wouldn't have dared to do at home. He'll kick over the traces that have held him for a long time and act as if he's never heard of justice, love or kindness. He becomes an insatiable beast!" These were the comments of a woman who had been an observer of this state of affairs in the lives of foreign men and women for more than twenty years. She had seen families broken-up by the anguish and tension arising out of the infidelity of the husband who no longer allowed himself to be ruled by a shrew. She had seen unscrupulous foreigners living apart from their families engaging in concubinage without the slightest qualms about what thee is meant to their families. She had witnessed her own private, intensely personal shattering blows of disillusionment that came from a husband who trampled upon the very sacred elements of her faith, trust, and love as he pursued the elixir of youth through numerous cities and country villages of Thailand and Southeast Asia. She had come to the point of bitter sarcasm and cynicism as she attempted to resurrect some philosophy of life from the shambles of her own disappointment. She had felt the heartache and despair of transplanting the roots of her life from the security and love of a small New England town where she knew everyone and everyone knew her, to the new, strange, bewildering life and customs of a land and culture totally foreign and alien to her. And then, after having carried out the painful process of learning the language, customs, traditions of a people who were very unlike her own, she had had the foundation of her new life in a new world cruelly uprooted and broken. Is it any wonder that there is despair? Is it at all strange that heartache, loneliness, bitter disappointment prevail when justice, trust, and love are abandoned in the search for anonymity, pleasure, and license to private desire?

Before you go on that trip to New York or Europe; before you go to that bar around the corner from your hotel where you're staying on a business trip; before you go into that new job or community where no one knows you and where you know no one; before you go with the boys or girls for a night on the town, before you go embarking on an adventure out of the present context of where you are into an opportunity of testing your freedom to choose what you like, permit me to prevail upon you to remember the lessons of this morning's scripture, a foundation is required upon which all else is built. Then no matter what new environment, customs, traditions we chance to come across, we are prepared to meet the new with expectant confidence that no matter what experience may befall us we shall not waiver and fall, but overcome the dangers even when the old familiar friends and environments no longer exist to keep us from the harm that might have been ours, but for them!

Before you go……is the preface of the most concerned and anxious remarks that anyone can make. Do you remember these words used by your wife, parents, husband or sweetheart before you lift for the Army and war? There was a catch in the throat as the word go was said and then the paroxysms of grief started without let up….. The haunting doubts of never returning; the anxiety of concern for your safety; the dangers involved in leavening the old and the familiar; the final gift or word or two as you embarked not knowing whether you would ever see each other again…..

Before you go…..the beginning of a statement that's never completed even when it is said. The letters that follow begin…..There was so much more I wanted to tell you….. There was so much left unsaid….."What I do and what I dream include thee, as the wine must taste of its own grapes. And when I see God for myself, He fears that name of thine, and sees within my eyes the tears of two."

Before you go…..into a new environment and become overwhelmed and perplexed by the differences and difficulties you encounter may I make these suggestions that may prove helpful in making the adjustment that has to be made if you are to maintain your sense of balance and profit from the experience rather than becoming a victim of it! If we have a grasp of the foundation that underlies all human activity then we need not fear what lies ahead. We can say with Browning,

> "Grow old along with me!
> The best is yet to be,
> The last of life, for which the first was made:

Our times are in his hand
Who saith, "A while I planned,
Youth shows but half; trust God: see all, be not afraid!
Then, welcome each rebuff
That turns earth's smoothness rough,
Each sting that bids nor sit nor stand but go!
Be our joys three–parts pain!
Strive, and hold cheap the strain;
Learn, nor account the pang;
Dare, never grudge the throe!
So, take and use thy work.
Amend what flaws may lurk,
What strain o'the stuff,
What war pings past the aim!
My times be in thy hand!
Perfect the cup as planned!
Let age approve of youth,
And death complete the same!

This is the first suggestion that I should make that each new situation we meet is a challenge to us; Teaching us to see how well we are able to conquer what would conquer us. In the tropics, the cycle of land use is clear, cultivate, harvest, and unless the challenge of clearing is taken up year by year there soon is nowhere to cultivate and nothing to be harvested. For the jungle will have taken over again. It's still a mystery what happened to the flourishing Hindu-Buddhist civilization built by Khmer warrior kings in central Cambodia. They had built the architectural wonders of Angkor Wat with its magnificent ornamental monuments, temples and palaces with 200 foot towers covering an area of over sixty square miles more than a thousand years ago. It flourished for 200 years and then…..

There was nothing to meet the challenge of the jungle and Angkor Wat was shrouded, overwhelmed, and absorbed by the impenetrable jungle where it remained hidden from the world until discovered by explorers late in the 19th century. The challenge was not met. The jungle conquered the life that should have conquered it!

Each new situation demands a response from us. Either we meet the challenge and adapt it to ourselves, or we have to adapt to it!

I've always been interested in calling on people who move into the parish. You can tell a great deal about the relative happiness or unhappiness that exists in a family by how they feel in their present environment. If they constantly bemoan the tragedy of having moved away from their old gang and neighborhood, you know that they've got problems far deeper than that of simply adjusting to new shopping centers, schools, bus lines, church, and neighbors. I wonder what it takes for a person to realize that they make moving additionally hard for themselves by their reluctance to think of it as an opportunity to meet new people, make new friends, have new experiences that can enrich their lives and life together as they have to wrestle with the problems of selling, moving, making new acquaintances? A woman told me some years ago of some mutual friends who simply had to move back to Fayetteville.....They just weren't happy until they had made their move back! As if Fayetteville, New York were the first, last, and only place on earth in which to live! And for those of you who've been elsewhere.....Honolulu, Nagasaki, Songkla, Pennang, Banduang, Innsbrueck.....You name the country and we'll name the place. Now, most of you in the congregation this morning I've known for a good many years. I appreciate your friendship very much and I hope I may have the privilege of continuing it throughout the coming years, but notice the persons who are sitting in the congregation this morning who know how to meet the challenge of the new.....With whom it's a joy to be with and who radiate this same kind of joy and interest not only here but at home, in their new community the sixth new one in which they've had to get acquainted!

Meeting the challenge of a new job, the new neighborhood, the new friends can be a rewarding and enriching experience. Before you go, remember it'll be a challenge calling you to respond!

Secondly, live by the highest values that you know. "Thou shalt love the Lord they God with all they heart, souls, mind and strength and they neighbor as thyself..... He has showed you, O man, what is good; and what does the Lord require of you, but to do justice, and to love kindness, and to walk humbly with thy God?"

Before you go.....remember the basis of your foundation, the anvil over which your new experiences will be hammered and molded into shape to your highest values. Some years ago a young married woman told me the decision she and her husband had made about drinking in their home.She said that before they got married she told him how she felt about it and he agreed. No liquor is kept in their home nor is it served when a party is given. Occasionally beer may be served to their guests but nothing more. And this is in a military setting at an American base in Germany. Mind you, drinking in Germany at parties has always been the case. The foundation had been well laid and was holding up despite the abundant activities to the contrary! They were living by their highest values.

The temptation to the contrary and to conform to the existing patterns of behavior are great. Wherever you go your highest values will be tested. You'll be offered abundant chances to be unfaithful; to be reckless with your money, your time and talents. For those of you who are going away to school in the Fall, into a new environment where your parents aren't going to be able to look over your shoulder and watch every move you make, you'll be testing your highest values on dates, at parties and in school. You'll either make the grade by wise use of your time and a study schedule or else you'll be among those twenty-five per centers who drop out and never finish. Each day may be an affirmation of what you are and hope to become or a denial of what you've learned and might be!

When you go out for a night on the town with your friends are you going to forget all about wife or your husband and the vows which you and your husband or wife made. Are you going to forget the vows you made and which your children follow because they understand why you made them to each other? It's always been a bit hard to understand how we obliterate from thought those imagines we dislike and only conjure up those that please us.....We dislike to see a young girl, with a haunted, hopeless expression in her eyes and a squalling baby in her arms.....a girl who doesn't know what she's going to do in the future or even knows if she'll have one; who lives from day to day in agony and remorse along with her struggles and memories which know no end.....We'd rather see a bright-eyed, cute young girl with a trim figure and intriguing dress.....It's always been a shock to see how often we only look on one side of a page; one side of our thoughts and actions and hurriedly suppress the other.....The consequences of what we do. Before you get familiar with that girl at the bar, or at the office, or at your client's store, are you looking at the whole picture? Are you considering her needs as a person; your wife's hope, trust and love; your children's future, their love and respect for you as their father? Before you go too far as yourself, are you living up to the highest values that you know? If you aren't, you're to be pitied. You'll never really know who you are nor why you lived! You'll be sitting down to a banquet of consequences instead of a feast of faith. Your attitude will be overshadowed by the clouds of doubt, dismay, and mistruth. Before you go thy way, all things say,

> Thou hast thy way to go, thou hast thy day to live;
> Thou hast thy need of thee to make
> In the hearts of others: do thy thing; yes awake
> The world's great thirst for yet another man!
> And be thou sure of this, no other can
> Do for thee that appointed thee of God:
> Nor any light shall shine upon they road
> For other eyes"
> Thee the angel calls.
> As he calls others; and thy life to thee
> Is devious as the greatest's life
> Can be to him;
> So live thy life and go thy way.

Before you go take everything you've learned and valued with you, apply it!

When Mahatma Gandhi returned ti India from South Africa in 1912, he was determined to do all that he could to gain the dignity, freedom, and the independence of his people from British rule. He had no army nor wealth with which to achieve these purposes. He had only an implicit faith that he could achieve his purposes if he were as honest with others as he was with himself. He wrote, "The British want us to put the struggle on the plane of machine-guns. They have weapons and we have not. Our only assurance of beating them is to keep it on the plane where we have weapons, and they have not. Our only assurance of beating them is to keep it on the plane where we have weapons and they have not." And thus Gandhi recognized the principle of nonviolence.....available to all, but used by few throughout the course of history. He may not have had much, but he used what he had with devastating effect!

When Louis Pasteur was a boy his school teacher wrote this about him: "He is the meekest, smallest, and least promising pupil in my class." He may have seemed like the weakest thing alive, but he certainly did use what he had with tremendous effect for the health of the world!

When Winston Churchill tried for the great British military academy of Sandhurst, he failed with exceptionally poor grades....He tried three times before he finally made it and then stood close to the bottom of his class. His professor made the remark to him on one occasion, "You'll surely never amount to very much. You're the poorest student I've ever seen!" He may not have been a very brilliant student, but he certainly used what he had to superb advantage!

Use what you have, my friends, use what you have..... We can wait a long, long time for the optimum conditions to arise, or for the most favorable circumstances to occur.....There are any number of people who dream and sigh for things to be just perfect, before they'll ever make any more or stir any effort to create what they would like to see happen. It reminds me of a group of young boys who used to play baseball in our back yard......One boy couldn't hit the ball very well and each time as he struck out he would burst into tears and finally after a few strike outs, he quit altogether.....saying I can't hit the ball anyway, so why should I keep playing? Think of it.....a young boy quitting baseball before he even got started! How will he ever learn to use what he has later if he doesn't make the attempt now?

We are continually facing this fact of life.....Will we use what we have? It's not only the so called great or important people who have to face this question.....It involves each one of us every day.....Will we worry about what ought to be or wish things were somehow different? Or will we recognize what we have and use it to the fullest extent possible?

Let us consider this morning the ways in which we may recognize what we have in order to use it to the best advantage.....

We need, first of all, to review our assets. When Gandhi made his decision to resist the British Government of India with passive resistance he had no doubt whatsoever concerning the righteousness of his cause.....In his correspondence with the great Russian writer, Leo Tolstoy, Gandhi's view of the principle of logic as the first law of life was confirmed by Tolstoy who identified nonviolence with Christianity and interpreted it as the universal law of the spirit. Therefore, because this was a universal law, Gandhi made nonviolence his absolute principle. "If I hit my adversary, that is, of course, violence; but to be truly non-violent, I must love him and pray for him even when he hits me." The only weapon, as one writer put it, that Gandhi and his followers had were: obedience, patience, forbearance, long suffering, courage, and good will. These were the means against which there was and is no victory…..for if faithfully and bravely served and carried out, it will win victory…..for if faithfully and bravely served and carried out, it will win in the end, for none other than God is on our side! The immeasurable assets of faith are ours to use, if we will but do so!!

It's evidently so close to us that we hardly recognize it…..We've somehow made love an obtuse and obscure thing in our lives…..We've let the rule of power and might dictate what should be done. We view love of neighbor as silly sentimentalism, but is it so silly? Then examine the alternatives to good will. Anger, ill will, resentment, violence, revenge, hatred…..and see what they are doing in the world!

Look at the harm done by hatred, not only to the one who is hated, but to the one who does the hating! One man of note has said, "If psychiatrists could get out of their patients the rancorous resentments, angers, and hatreds that have accumulated there, they could well nigh empty half of their hospitals. One psychiatrist has written: "Hatred is truly the arch demon of all the little devils who are subversive of joy and destructive of happiness."

One of the things a person should do on occasion is write down his/her assets. Make a list of what he/she has that he/she may begin to realize what he/she has lest he/she take them for granted. It's exactly the same principle as that involved before making a decision…..You'd be amazed how often people make decisions simply on the basis of whim or fancy. They don't stop to think or analyze if it's the right decision by writing down the assets and liabilities of their decision. I'm not suggesting that this idea be carried to an extreme. I knew a missionary years ago who came back to this country on a furlough with a list of requirements of what his prospective wife should be and have. He was determined to find the one who matched these essential characteristics before he returned to his mission post. Each time he met a girl to whom he seemed attracted he'd check over his list of qualifications......If she didn't match his list he'd stop dating her. I understand from friends of his that when he met the girl and finally married her......He didn't try to match the girl on his hide list. Instead, he listed her assets and found himself seeing that when he met the girl he finally married her....He didn't try to match the girl to his hide list. Instead, he listed her assets and found himself seeing qualities in her his list of qualifications hadn't carried......

This is the real value of drawing up a list of assets first, so that you can set them when you find something far greater that you ever expected!

Let us review our assets, my friends, in order to begin to see how we may best use what we have.

The second way in which we may see how to use what we have is to examine our problems or difficulties in light of what we have. At an Official Board meeting at my church years ago, the question was raised concerning what would happen to the 100 odd names of people who we removed from our membership rolls at our Quarterly Conference. "Why remove people from our membership rolls anyway, the question came up? Aside from the fact that these people had simply vanished from any possibility of contact was this additional reason, the church as an organization could only exist through the participation and support of its members. And while it appeared that we would meet our conference obligations this year. A church of our size didn't need to carry a yearly deficit if each one of our members would fulfill their membership obligations. Examining our perennial financial problems in light of the membership we had, we still found almost ninety families who had not made any effect whatsoever to fulfill their accepted financial obligation as members of this church.

In view of the yearly financial problems which we've had in this church, here is an obvious area where we might well make much better use of what we have. We wouldn't be at all hard pressed and could well do far more if each one of us accepted his/her share of the responsibility involved. I may make myself very unpopular for these views but we should make every effort possible this next year to arouse not only greater participation, but also support on the part of those who are inactive and delinquent members. There's real value in sharing not only our difficulties, but in arousing an awareness of what is going on and the part we play in it.

One of the most humbling experiences I've found that I have had is from visits to some of our church "shut-ins". Here are people who have very little income and yet they give entirely beyond their means because they feel a strong loyalty and obligation to support their church. I used to have some doubts concerning letters that were sent out last Fall to members who were still listed on our membership rolls, but who had not shown an inclination to share in the support of our church. But after visiting some of our "shut-ins" recently and receiving donations for the church which they insisted upon giving, I no longer feel any qualms concerning the justification of those letters.....I cannot feel humbled by their obvious sacrifice in doing so much with the little that they have while there are so many of us who are doing so little with the great amount that we have.

Just this past week a woman called protesting her inability to pay for the removal of some sub-standard housing that she owns. She just couldn't afford it. She only lives in a fifty thousand dollar home.....

It's a real tragedy when we fail to examine our difficulties in light of what we have.....

The final suggestion is that we should capitalize on our assets. The story is told that when President Lincoln proposed U. S. Grant to become Chief of Staff of the Northern Armies there were violent outbursts against the appointment because Grant allegedly drank too much..... Lincoln was fed up with the constant harping upon Grant's drinking while ignoring the fact of his fearless courage in leading his men into battle after battle. After another protest committee came to Lincoln he dispensed with his critics by saying, "Find out the brand he drinks so that I can apply it to all my generals. Perhaps it'll put the same kind of brilliance and courage into them as General Grant has...." This is not to say that Lincoln condoned drinking. He himself was a teetotaler. He saw, however, what others evidently did not see. A man who had infinite capabilities and assets that could be put to good use despite his handicaps or liabilities. Let's just bring this closer home a bit.....How many of us would be automatically rejected for certain kinds of endeavors for a variety of reasons. Because our health is bad, or because we smoke too much, or because of a violent temper that gets the better of us on occasion, or because of periods of prolonged depression, or because of insomnia or fitful sleeping habits.....They may not seem like much but for certain types of jobs or responsibilities we would be automatically eliminated. If you've filled out any forms of any kind recently you may recall the highly technical personal information that is desired. Things like smoking, drinking, overweight, insomnia, depression, etc. all are key indicators that reveal a lot to a trained psychologist or physician about your personal make-up. Not many of us could stand the type of scrutiny required for certain tasks…..However, most of us have enough other assets that far overshadow some of these disabilities…..It is these issues that we need to capitalize upon and yet we often fail to see what is closest at hand. Take this matter of attending college, for example. How often we find almost total blindness on the part of students or their parents when it comes to picking a school. There's one dear lady who lives in another state, Pennsylvania, to be exact. Her son is a really intelligent boy who wished to study civil engineering……Located not more than ninety miles from his home, is one of the finest educational institutions in the entire country, Penn State, to be exact where he could study tuition free as a Pennsylvania resident. So where does he go? Seven hundred miles away to small Catholic University in Wisconsin because his mother wanted him to get a "Catholic Education"…Hardly an example of capitalizing on an unparalleled educational asset right in his own back yard! There are other examples too, where the closet, the obvious, is neglected while students go off on a lark of passing interest that changes from year to year, month to month.

If we could only capitalize on our assets or at least recognize that they are there waiting to be discovered, tapped, used if we will but do so! What was it Paul said, "A little yeast leavens the whole lump?"

Karl limped when he walked…..One of his hands had two missing fingers…..There were three other scars that he would bear for the rest of his life…..But Karl was only one of three men out of a class of thirty who was still alive…. He had been in the German Army for six years in World War II, but as he said of himself…..at least, I'm alive…..

If only we could realize, we have at our very doors the ultimate opportunity that God has given to each one of us.....Life with its radiant possibility of faith, hope and love.....This is the greatest asset of all.....

Loose In The World

In John Masefield's poetic drama "The trial of Jesus, "Procula", the wife of Pilate, is deeply concerned over the crucifixion of Jesus. A Roman soldier, Longinus, comes to report that he has found the tomb of Jesus empty. Pilate's wife asks, in great excitement, "Do you believe his claim?"Longinus answered, "If a man believes anything up to the point of dying on a cross for it he will find others to believe it." But Procula persists: "Do you believe it?" Longinus answers reflectively:"He was a fine young fellow, my Lady, not past middle age. And he was alone and defied all the Jews and the Romans, and when we had done with him he was a poor broken down thing, dead on the cross." Procula still presses Longinus for an answer: "Do you think he is dead?" And finally Longinus answers: "No, Lady, I don't." Procula asks; "Then where is he?" Longinus replies, "Loose in the world, Lady, where neither Jew nor Roman can stop his truth!"

Loose in the world, my friends, loose in the world! This is the great pronouncement of Easter. That God's spirit is loose in the world where nothing can separate it from us…..Where no single event, experience, or expression can ever be without his abiding presence about, within, or beyond it.

The message of that first Easter was that of a coming back, a returning back into a notice just when all the disciples, the religious authorities, the Romans, and the crowds thought he was gone once and for all time. The disciples thought they had lost their great friend and teacher, the authorities thought they had gotten rid of a perniciously upsetting sect; the Romans thought they had put down a possible rebellion; and the crowd thought they had heard the last of this pretender who had died so ignobly upon a cross. But all of them were to discover that he was still very much loose in the world! For some persons to be a nemesis that was to plague them for the rest of their days, and for others an overwhelming affirmation of the goodness of God.

The message of this Easter and of every Easter since has been and is, he is very much "loose in the world!"

Let us consider the meaning of Easter this morning in light of this overwhelming affirmation that he lives; that he is loose in the world! He cannot be contained. One of the first meanings that this day of Easter has is that behind today lies tomorrow.

There is no single event that can ever encompass everything that exists. Dr. Howard Thurman, Dean of the Boston University Chapel put it another way when he said, "Life is a movement on an isthmus between two continents. Each person is on a pilgrimage from one world to the next." From today to tomorrow. Have you ever stopped to think how much of a creature or space we are? We think in terms of places when we think of ourselves or someone else…..The kind of a house a person lives in; the street on which it's located; the city of which it is a part; the type of countryside in which it's located…..We think of ourselves in terms of space. The place we occupy at a particular instance. The event which occurs at such and such a place on a particular kind of a day. We are creatures of space in our thought patterns, in our estimates of ourselves......

If you are driving down a busy street and you're anxious to go somewhere and you find one driver who seems obstinately slow and straddles two lanes you immediately label him in terms of space-----"That road hog! Why doesn't he move over?" Or if go shopping on a particular day before Christmas or Easter you find yourself buffeted around from counter to counter in the stores and you say, "Gee, the stores were too crowded today." It's another way of reflecting our spatial concepts. We mean we've had to struggle for our particular area of space on earth that day! We're very much creatures of space. We measure the meaning of our lives in terms of events or spatial happenings that take place. But we're also creatures of time. We said just a moment ago how aggravated we become when someone gets in our way spatially, especially when we must be spatially in another place at a specific time. Then there's a real conflict within us between time and space; Our time and someone else's space! We realize the necessity of time, however, the modes of thought can sometimes be in momentary conflict with each other until time and space are reconciled with each other. Although we are of necessity creatures having to reconcile time with space, we are, in another sense, beyond this immediate need of space-time reconciliation. We may stand in time outside of spatial events. We may stand beyond the facts of our existence or beyond our own immediate experience. Have you ever noticed how often people remain only on the space-time continuum? "I'll never go and see her again! Why, do you know what she said to me?" And from that moment of time, this person, no matter how long a period of time passes is still back there, in the past, at that ancient moment of time with the same spatial view in mind of the situation and of how it occurred and how she felt.....She's trapped; physically, spatially and, time-wise, mentally in a period of time long since past and all that has gone on since that slight or insult even while participating spatially in other events time wise, she had remained, "back there."

One of the real difficulties resulting from the death of a loved one is that of those who remain among the living. Remaining time wise in those joyous moments of the past where the love and fellowship of the one who has gone is mistakenly thought to be continued. So that each new experience is forever weighted and limited by the past. While we may be creatures unfortunately locked in time, we may also see time as a fragment of eternity. These moments are not completely of and for themselves. This single moment of time never stands alone. It represents the results of the past as well as the consequences of the future. There is never a moment that stands alone. It is materially linked with the past and the future...Think of what it means to face a particular obstacle in time. Do you recall how you felt when you were ill or when you suffered that accident? At first you were almost totally in the situation. You neither thought of the past nor wondered about the future. You were completely absorbed in the moment of time. Then, as the severity of the moment subsided you began to go back in time to reconstruct what happened. You tried to recapture everything that preceded that particular moment of time. Then you began to look ahead in time, trying to envision what might lie ahead..... Trying to see what this experience might mean for you in the future. And slowly you began to make your peace with the past while preparing yourself for the future with the necessary adjustments you would have to make for your temporary condition of pain and agony and some permanent changes of life that you only have barely begun to understand, yet already beyond today you can see lies tomorrow. Beyond the limits of these moments are the opportunities of tomorrow, different, severe even, but there to be discovered as the mind ranges over the past and learns to anticipate the future.....

The second discovery we can find in Easter is that beyond the event lies its meaning. We can never fully understand what is happening while it occurs. To return fork a moment to the last illustration, we know for example that reckless or drunken driving may result in a very severe or even fatal accident. Yet we do not know exactly what the event will mean in each person's life at the moment of its occurrence or even directly following it. It's meaning is gradually worked out as thought is applied upon what has taken place.

The late Professor Collingwood, of Oxford University, had this to say about the late discovery of the meaning of events. He wrote, "Civilizations die as they are born. Not with the waving of flags or with the noise of machine guns in the streets. But in the stillness, in the darkness, when no one is aware of it." Only years later, someone looking back realizes that it has happened." The meaning always follows the event.

If we examine the scriptural record of what happened at the crucifixion, we find that none of the disciples discovered the meaning of the event while it was taking place. Indeed, it was a Roman centurion who at least recognized what no one else seemed to: "Truly this man was a son of God!" Even with all of the preparation Jesus had made for his disciples in telling them he was to die, they still did not understand what had happened. But scarily three days after the event, we find the amazing perception being realized by the disciples that there was something everlastingly true about their experience with Jesus that, therefore, even the finality of the event of crucifixion had a tremendous meaning for each of their lives…..that if he should be willing to show them how to live and die because of his overwhelming belief and trust in God could they do anything less than what he did? Could there be anything less than that? Beyond the event lay the meaning which transformed them from ignorant, crude fishermen into men with a powerful and dynamic faith which shook the foundations of the Roman Empire itself and each one was to find himself put to death in equally as gruesome a manner as their teacher.

I suppose at this point it would be appropriate to go into a long theological discourse about the way in which the interpretation of the meaning of the disappearance of the body from the tomb has become the disappointment of Christian history for some of us. But I won't. This is an article of faith that I shall leave to your own judgment. I shall only say as one of our New Testament Professors said in a class in Seminary….."The only thing Christian Scholars can agree upon is that the tomb was empty." This was the event…..the meaning lay beyond this fact and we may interpret this as we like. We acknowledge the fact….. the event…..of the empty tomb, but when it comes to the meaning, this is where we begin to quarrel.

It is enough for us to say that beyond the event lies the meaning…..the meaning does not arise first to be followed by events…..This is only in the era of speculation. The facts are what reality is based upon and these must be sorted out and sifted through for their meaning. One of the great achievements of modern psychoanalysis is in the field of therapy. In counseling a counselor and the counseled have to go through the events and experiences that have occurred in the life of the counseled, some of which may have occurred a long time ago in an order the counseled may begin to discover for himself/herself the meaning these experiences and events have had and which he/she have never been able to interpret constructively. It's a process of sifting through and sorting out events until new patterns of meaning form which the person has not considered before. Beyond the event lies the meaning sometimes years later and, fortunate is the man who is able to gain insight into the meaning of events that have occurred within his lifetime.

The final meaning that Easter has is that beyond experience lies God. We've said that we are creatures of space and of time. But we are also creatures of experience. We hear it said quite frequently, we have to test ideas or propositions by experience or experience is the best teacher. But let's not make the mistake of thinking our experience is supreme.....that there is nothing higher than it. If this were true, we would all dwell on our own little islands of experience and forget that is is only when the sum of them is put together with others that experience can really be considered a valid criterion of truth. Think of the experience represented here this morning by each one of us! The loss of a husband at an early age; the birth of a malformed infant; the agony of watching a child struggle with a crippling disease; the pain of seeing a loved one waste away before our very eyes with the scourge of cancer; the nagging heartache and loneliness that comes from watching a husband run off with an unscrupulous strumpet all body and no head; the bitterness of being rejected by one whom we trusted and thought our friend; the shattering dismay in finding out our parents are not the paragons of virtue and goodness we thought them to be; the constant battle with the bottle that saw a splendid person degenerate into an empty shell of a mate! What would happen if each one of us had only his/her experience to trust? We should shortly go mad or dwell in utter defeat and dejection for the rest of our days! No! If our experience tells us anything it is that experience alone is not enough! We see too many people who trust only their own experience and dwell in the obstructing narrowness of their misery for they believe that life represents only the total of what they've experienced! But look instead again to this overwhelming affirmation of Easter.....that beyond even the most searing, heartrending, crucifying experiences we can have lies God.

Look at what this belief beyond experience did for the early Christians.....It enabled them to withstand the torture, the bestiality, the tearing apart by wild beasts, the burnings, the stoneings, the maimings of those who thought that if they were only severely enough treated, or beaten, or brutally murdered then their faith would not be stamped out,,,,,And yet, the whole affirmation of Christian history is that even beyond the worst experiences or of death lies God. The story of Easter screams this out.....that there is no single expression nor experience of life that exhausts life! What was it that Paul said, "For I am persuaded that neither death nor life, nor angels, not principalities, nor things present, not things to come, nor powers nor heights, nor depth, nor anything else in all creation, will be able to separate us from the love of God......!"

Beyond experience lies God…..
"I am a part of all that I have met;
Yet all experience is an arch wherethro'
Gleams that untravelled world, whose margin fades,
For ever and for ever when I move.

Life is not through even in death. He's loose in the world, my friends, loose in the world!

How Easily Forgotten

"**M**en don't spend their time thanking God for cars; they only curse when they've carburetor is choked." Aldous Huxley wrote this statement in 1933. It could have been written just as easily this morning or even a few days ago. I had a flat tire some days ago and do you know what my first reaction was?

Men don't spend their time thanking God for what they have; they only curse when things don't go their way! We seem to think that each day should run smoothly; that is just the way we want it and if it doesn't…..Ladies, the next time you and your husband decide at the last minute to take that overnight trip or visit friends for a while before the children have to go to bed and then run into a traffic jam or snow storm, just make a mental note of what your husband says…..I'd suggest making a mental note of it, for your own sakes…..

"We don't spend our time thanking God for what we have; we only curse when things don't go our way!"

And the psalmist wrote, "Bless the Lord, O my soul, and forget not all of his benefits." Forget not all of his benefits, yet how easily forgotten are his many benefits to us….. Perhaps it's the sheer complexity of modern life which is such an aide to forgetting. I read in a magazine several years ago where New York City had such an interlocking network of communications, utilities, and transportation lines that it took a serviceman from one of the departments approximately nine months before he knew where all of the outlets were in his district! The amazing complexity of a city is symbolic of the complexity of modern life. But we are not the first to have had this feeling. The ancient Judeans used to view their northern brethren of Samaria with critical eyes too. They thought of them as too worldly.....Too much concerned with the daily elements of filching to be reverent enough about life. The big modern cities of ancient Israel were to the north of the Judean hills, with entirely too much contact with foreigners and too much thought for this world.

What we take for granted would have overwhelmed our grandparents or great grandparents. The last fifty years have seen more inventions and scientific discoveries made than in all of the rest of human history put together! Fifty years verses ten thousand years! What a tremendously alive and challenging period of history this is in which we live! Yet, how easily we forget all of his benefits!

We may have forgotten his benefits every day at home. We forgot his benefits every day in school. We forget his benefits every day at work.....We forget his benefits every day in so many ways. Benefits which we take for granted having been born into them which is the case with those of us who are young or soon taken for granted by those who are older.

"Bless the Lord, O my soul, and forget not all of his benefits." Can you recall Thanksgiving in 1961? How easily forgotten are his daily benefits to us.....May we be reminded of the opportunities we have had that we might be truly grateful and give thanks for our blessings? I should like to consider with you our many benefits in light of what Thanksgiving ought to mean to us. For what should we be thankful?

One of the first reminders we need is to give thanks for the very gift of life itself! When the Pilgrims established their first Thanksgiving in 1621 according to Webster's New World Dictionary, they did so in order to "give thanks to God for their survival!" I wouldn't want to question the reliability of the source, but if that's the case then our view today is, I should hope, quite different. To thank God for survival has the implication of "I'm glad I made it! Too bad about the others which is hardly the Christian meaning we would like to engender today..... We don't give thanks for being spared the agony, pain, and suffering that comes from the loss of a loved one..... There is no sparing of the reality of death whether young or old.....We've seen it happens altogether too often where someone has prayed and prayed for their son to be spared on the battlefield, or for their wife to survive her illness, or for a father to recover from a heart attack only to become disappointed and embittered, blaming God for their own broken desires! There's far too much of this blaming God for our own immaturity. At a Bel-Air fire in Hollywood, California years ago which destroyed a number of homes of Hollywood stars one of them was heard to say, "It must have been the hand of God that saved ours from destruction." A foreman standing nearby was heard to say, "You might give some credit to the firemen who saved it, too!"

How true it is, we do not give thanks for the gift of life! It is for the raw materials of mind, body, and resources out of which we've fashioned a world of our own choosing!

It is God from whom we have received these gifts and to whom we own our thanks for these opportunities.

A Seminary professor who taught Philosophy of Religion raised an extremely acute point of view in our minds many years ago. We had our last class before the Thanksgiving vacation and we had been talking about responsibility. He said, "I hope you don't sit down to a lush turkey dinner tomorrow, give thanks to God for all of the blessings you have, and then stuff yourselves so that can hardly move for the rest of the day!" He went on to say, "I can't think of anything more sacrileges or self-contradictory than this when we know there are people who haven't even enough food to live while we have more than is good for us!"

Our task is not so much physical survival as it is a survival of appreciation, gratitude, and thanksgiving for the gift of life that we have.

Our second reminder is to remember the sacrifices of the past that have made the present possible. During one of Emperor Hadrian's many travels to distant parts of the Roman Empire he and his party one day came upon the scene of an old man digging a trench in which to plant fig trees. The Emperor stopped and called to the man. "If you had spent your youth in better labor, you might now not have to labor so hard in your old age."

The old man looked up and said he had labored well throughout his lifetime and had nothing to regret. Hadrian asked him how old he was and the man replied "Near 100." The Emperor asked in gentle mockery, "Dost Thou think Thou shalt taste the fruit of these trees?" The old man replied.

"Perhaps, but has not my father planted trees the fruit of which I eat today and shall I then not plant trees for my children?"

Hadrian was so well pleased with the old man's answer that he invited him to the palace if he should ever see the fruit ripening. The story ends with the old man bringing the emperor a basket of fruit and the emperor gave him a basket of gold in exchange.

Whether the story is fact or fiction, is immaterial. What the old man did and the reason why he did it was the story of mankind in miniature. Shall we not do for our children as our parents have done for us? Our parents need not have saved so diligently to see us to school, but they did! Our parents need not have bought houses and gone into debt in order to provide us with homes, but they did! Our parents need not have tolerated our youthful anger and open disagreement, but they did! Our parents need not have allowed difference of thought and independent pursuit of interests, but they did! Our parents need not have loved us through the sorrows and hardships we may have caused them, but they did!

The sacrifices of the past are what have made the present possible.....For all that we are and have we own an immeasurable debt of gratitude to those who have gone before us.

And the final reminder for this season of Thanksgiving is to remember that we are the keys to the doors of the future. As the past has made the present possible, so too, today determines tomorrow. Thanksgiving often becomes a passive time. It's often a time stopper. There's no work except for the wives and mothers of the families as they get together; friendships renewed; stock taken of all of our blessings.....It's a time to recharge our batteries in a sense. Unless we forget that this recharge is to be used in the days ahead to look to the future of the significance of Thanksgiving.

It was Albert Einstein who once said, "A hundred times a day I remind myself that my inner and outer life depends on the labors of other men, living and dead, and that I must exert myself in order to give in the same measure as I have received and am receiving. Thanksgiving is a continuing process not only of remembering the past, but of a rededication to the future. Some people feel they have to control the present pretty closely in order to insure the future they envision. It reminds me of s story Professor Harold Bosley once told about his Yale graduate, who took his son to enroll at his old alma mater. He had heard rumors about new ways and ideas there, so he sought out the Dean of Students and told him his dream for the boy: "I want him to get exactly what I got when I was here." The Dean puzzled for a moment and then asked, "You mean you want him to follow in your footsteps?" The father smilingly agreed.The Dean said, "Look, now! You're a great guy and we're proud of you, but don't you think one of you is enough?" It's not this kind of a future we want, simply a repeat of what we already have…..But a future which is even more graphic, more complete than anything experienced in the past.

We are the keys to the doors of the future. What we believe, say, and do can be the key by which the doors of a person's life may open to a future they themselves could not have expected. Probably the most pathetic note that we hear sounded these days is the note of disappointment because people feel they don't count for much. Their lives are empty of meaning when just the opposite is the case for good or ill.

Will Rogers was asked one day what he thought was wrong with the world and he drawled "Well, I dunno. I guess its people." That's it, people like you and me who are the keys that unlock the doors of the future for our families, our friends, and our neighbors......

What would happen if no one volunteered to shoulder another's burden? What would happen if the well did not care for the sick? What would happen if a doctor refused to go to the aid of the injured or the diseased? What would happen if we closed the door of our hearts each time our children did something we did not like? What would happen if a wife did not stick by her husband after he got into financial or personal difficulty? What would happen if there were no recourse to reconciliation where injustice was perpetrated? What would happen?

We are the keys that unlock the doors of the future for others even as they unlock them for us. Dr. F. W. Norwood, an Australian minister who asked a man to consider the consequences of his actions in the life of his family was brusquely turned aside and told to mind his own business. It wasn't too many months later, however, when the man began coming to church and even desired to join it. Dr. Norwood asked him what made him change his mind so completely. He said, "You know I have a little boy. A week or so as I was taking him for a walk in the country when we came to a rather rugged pathway where we had to walk single file. I was going on ahead and had forgotten that the lad was finding the way a little more difficult than myself. Suddenly, I heard his small voice say: "Be careful where you step, Daddy, I'm coming behind you. That settled it.....I want to join the Church." Let's be careful where we step, my friends, there are others coming behind us. We are the keys that unlock the doors of the future for our families, friends, and neighbors.

And the psalmist wrote, "Bless the Lord, O my soul, and forget not all of his benefits, who forgives all our iniquity, who heals all of our diseases, who redeems our lives from evil, who crowns us with steadfast love and mercy, who satisfies us with good as long as we live."

In Passing

"**I** hope to see you in passing as I go to Spain." Paul's life is a story of movement: From one experience to another; from one kind of a life to another. From one place to another; from one period of time to another. Paul's life is the epitome of movement; passing from one event to another throughout his lifetime. He was born in the city of Tarsus in the family of a well to do Jew. He lived in a city that was one of the finest centers of higher education in the world of this time, only Athens and Alexandria could rival Tarsus as a university and cultural center. Tarsus was a cross-road for caravans and trade from all parts of the Roman Empire. It was situated at a key spot for all land routes between East and West, controlling one of the finest harbors in the world as swell as the main route through the mountainous interior of Asia Minor.

Education was stressed for young Saul. Not only the University was of great influence upon him as a boy attending the public forums and thus hearing some of the greatest scholars of this age, but also the education that comes from living in a cosmopolitan city where there is daily mingling with scores of people from many countries all speaking several languages in communicating with each other. Saul couldn't help but be influenced by such a rich cultural setting, He undoubtedly learned several languages through this process of early exposure, languages he would later put to good use in his journeys from country to country.

Although his father was well-to-do, he was nevertheless obligated by Jewish Law to teach his son a trade of some sort. Thus it was that Saul learned tent making, useful later also as he made his way across the Roman world with no means other than what his hands and friends could provide for him.

After his studies in Tarsus, he was sent by his father to study in Jerusalem under the great rabbinic teacher Gamaliel. Saul was soon acknowledged even by his fellow Jews to be an outstanding student.

His familiarity with Greek thought and his easy command of the content of the Jewish scriptures was later reflected in his letters and must have impressed his teacher and fellow students tremendously. He was later to quote from over 141 different chapters of scripture and over 200 single verses of scripture.

His scholastic preeminence and religious enthusiasm may have led to his appointment as the Rabbi of a synagogue. It was during this time that he heard the testimony of the Christians examined before the synagogue. Saul had been chosen by the Jewish religious authorities, the Sanhedrin, to stamp out the Nazarene movement among the Jews. It was during this time that he carried out his systematic destruction of them when he witnessed the sting of Stephen. Through all of these events Saul was carrying out a strict, legal interpretation of the law. But he began to hear repeatedly how lives had been altered by their new experience of having known the Nazarene. There was something more than rules to follow.

Here was experience that people had had which changed their lives completely. He couldn't help but think of these people and what they said before being beaten to death.

The more Saul heard; the more he reacted against it. He set out in deliberate pursuit of the Christians to try to stamp them out. Because of the severity of his persecutions the Christians scattered to other less dangerous cities and towns in Palestine. Saul set out in pursuit of these fleeing Nazarenes asking for letters from the high priest in Jerusalem addressed to other synagogues which would allow him the right to continue his examinations and persecutions of Nazarenes in other cities. With these letters of condemnation, a troop of religious witch hunters, and his own accumulating doubts concerning the legitimacy of the religious law in the face of the mere faith in the Nazarene declared by his disciples, Saul set forth from Jerusalem to Damascus.

As he travelled with his assistants, Paul was lost in thought. He remembered Stephen and how he hadn't resisted his fate but had accepted it. Saul may have remembered the likeness between Stephen and the Nazarene whom he may have seen die on the cross. Suddenly the idea flashed across Saul's mind, the great scholar and highly religious pharisee, yet eminently practical man suddenly had the idea cross his mind that Jesus was the suffering Messiah noted in Isaiah's writings!!

The severity of the shock was so great that Saul was overcome in an epileptic seizure. The contrast between what he was doing and should have done never left him completely. He had caused the death of innocent men, women, and children the guilt from which he was never to find complete relief; the guilt of his own sin continued with him until he too was finally killed. And thus, Saul, the rabbinic scholar, the staunch legalistic pharisee, and the persecutor of the Christians he became one of them. He was no longer able to carry the ancient, traditional name, Saul, but instead, the Roman name of Paul. Almost if the change in name was symbolic of the change in faith and for the balance of his life, to be a missionary among those who were not even Jews, but to any man who might listen, learn, and lead this same new life that Paul had experienced.

This was only the beginning for Paul of a life that was ever in a state of passing. He exemplified the sort of life we need to recognize as the condition of all of us; in constant movement in passing from one aspect of life to another.

There are three phases to this state of being which Paul fulfilled so well. The first phase is that of passing from one experience to another. For Paul, it was perfectly natural to pass from the public forums of Tarsus to the lectures and discussion of the university. It was relatively simple for him to debate with his fellow rabbinical students or the Athenians because of the early exposure to some of the greatest orators of his day. It was possible for him to gain employment no matter where he went because he had a trade. He could use his hands as skillfully as he could his tongue. He could meet one difficult experience after another because of his trusting confidence that no matter what assailed him, noting could separate him from the love of God as he had seen it in Jesus. No experience was too great for him. No experience was too hard or bitter for him.....Each experience was taken in passing as a demonstration of God's power within his life.

How true is this of us? Are we as confident and trusting in life as we pass from one experience to another? Take this matter of crises; how stable are we in our ability to meet them? Or do we go to pieces, fearful for ourselves and, therefore, unable to function; breaking down without the intention of salvaging what we can from the ability to struggle that much harder and inspire the loss or handicap?

Frankie wasn't very big but he had lots of spirit and was as tough as anyone on the team. He played halfback with distinction although the coach usually worried about him. He tried to use him sparingly. He said he wasn't really heavy enough to play football. But Frankie played, nevertheless. He didn't want to be on the sidelines. He wanted to play just like anyone else. He played a terrific game of baseball as a center fielder making all of this catches one-handed as if he were playing to the grandstand. He never hit any home runs, but was a consistent hitter, striking out very few times in two years of varsity ball. Anyone hearing of Frankie's feats one would think he was a real fine athlete, which he was, with a strong well developed physique, which was partially true. But Frankie was a superbly developed one-armed player. He lost his right arm just above the elbow in an automobile accident as a young boy. It could have been an insufferable loss, but he turned his handicap into immense gain by developing his body and remaining arm into more than enough to make up for the loss of his right arm!

As we go from one experience to another, how do we meet the ensuing crisis? How well do we accept the ups and downs of experience in passing?

The second phase of Paul's life from which we may draw courage and strength is by observing what he did in passing from one kind of life to another. It was not easy for Paul to renounce his entire upbringing. It was not easy for him to condemn the law as too limited to encompass the meaning of life. It was not easy for him to be rejected by the Sanhedrin and his fellow rabbis. It made him a professional outcast among his colleagues. Everything for which he once stood he now saw how mistaken he had been. He was still proud of being a Jew. He still called himself a Hebrew among Hebrews because of his family and heritage. He was still proud of his Roman citizenship and used it whenever necessity demanded it such as at Philippi and Jerusalem. He was proud of his schooling and the tradition of rigorous scholarship to which he had been exposed…..but he was willing to forego these privileges of position, power and prestige to join a small band of persecuted, illiterates whose sole claim to fame was that they had had an unforgettable encounter with a man whose very words and conduct had changed their lives.

What about ourselves? How willing are we to forsake the comforts and conveniences of daily life to give voice to the unvoiced need for justice and fair-play in our dealings with one another to say nothing of doing so with minority groups within our midst; to give demonstration to the fact that we can live in harmony with those of another race or religion. How many of us are willing to endure the taunts and insults of our friends and neighbors in order to help those displaced from one ward to the next to be moved? How many of us are willing to leave the old life of prejudice, bigotry, and hatred behind as Paul did to pass into a life of tolerance, neighborliness, and good will to all men and women? This is what Paul did as he said, "that we may grow up into his likeness in all things." How ready are we in passing from one kind of a life to another?

And finally, the third phase of Paul's life represents his passing from out of the pages of history into daily life. This is the distinctive mark of any great person of history….that he/she would have the ability of stepping out of the pages of history unto any street, or home, or place of employment and deal with a given situation in exactly the same manner as Paul had done. The issues of history are always the same, the characters are different, the scenes have modern settings, but strife, factions, controversies, quarrels…..the essentials of poor interpersonal relations continue.

Paul had one continuing quarrel after another with some of the churches he had established. There was jealousy, bickering, struggle for leadership, immorality, hatred, etc. all of the features that make up the daily life of a contemporary church as well as in Paul's day and even among the very earliest religious groups of humankind. The issues were the same, the principles different. Paul could confront the same issues in any number of congregations today even as he did then…..He transcended history…..He was a perpetual part of his time.

What about ourselves? Do we see ourselves as a perpetual part of time? Can we see where we may pass from history to the future present? We may if we recognize the influence we may have on the present.

> "Hold high the torch!
> You did not light its glow.
> 'Twas given you by other hands, you know.
> "Tis yours to keep it burning bright,
> Yours to pass on when you no more need light;"
> I think it started down its pathway bright,
> The day the Maker said, "Let there be light!"
> And He, once said, who hung on Calvary's tree
> "Ye are the light of the world. Go shine for me!"
> And Paul said, "I hope to see you in passing….."

From Peak To Peak

In Aldous Huxley's book "Eyeless in Gaza" he has his two main characters, Anthony and Helen, discussing the problem of hatred and a possible remedy for it.

Helen says, "But most people are detestable."

Anthony replies, "They're detestable because we detest them. If we liked them, they'd be likable."

"Do you think that's true?"

"I'm sure it's true."

"And what do you do after that?"

"There's no after," he replied, "Because, of course, it's a lifetime's job.....Every time you get to the top of a peak, you see another peak in front of you.....a peak that you couldn't see from lower down.....The ideal ends recede as you approach them. They're seen to be other and more remarkable than they seemed before the advance was begun. It's the same when one tries to change one's relations with other people. Every step forward reveals the necessity of making new steps forward...... .....unanticipated steps, towards a destination one hadn't seen when one set out.

As children we often sang a rather simple ditty that grossly distorted reality. It went, "The bear went over the mountain, the bear went over the mountain, the bear went over the mountain to see what he could see. And all that he could see was the other side of the mountain, was all that he could see."

Perhaps the composer of the lyric tried to describe how a bear felt or more likely, how he himself felt, but that's not all that a person finds climbing mountains! It's true, he does see the other side of the mountain but he also sees scenes of unparalleled beauty, breath-taking panoramas of nature, awe inspiring views of a horizon and the privileged glimpses of what life is like on the other side of the mountain. For mountain climbing is a process of continually moving from peak to peak as we conquer one prominence after another on our way up to the top. And then when we finally reach the top, we find not an ending or difficulties or an edge of the world view, but rather a continuation of what we've already gone through. We go from peak to peak throughout or lifetimes.

In Aldous Huxley's book, "Eyeless in Gaza" the two leading characters, Anthony and Helen, are discussing ways in which to overcome hatred. After Anthony suggests trying to find people likeable, Helen asks "And what do you do after that?" Anthony replied, "There's no after, because, it's a lifetime job.....Every thine you get to the top of a peak, you see another peak in front of you.....a peak you couldn't see from lower down.....The ideal ends and recedes as you approach them. They're seen to be other and more remarkable than they seemed before the advance was begun.Every step forward reveals the necessity of making new steps forward.....unanticipated steps, towards a destination one hadn't seen when one set out."

From step to step, from height to height, from peak to peak. We move and not only do we find ourselves in a different time and space sequence, but in a different relationship with life itself!

In the scriptures we have the unmistakable call of God to man to rise to the peaks of wisdom and understanding. We hear it often, don't we, that we simply cannot climb the heights of such high spiritual insight in order to follow in the footsteps of the prophets, Jesus and the Apostles. The verse from the 139th psalm summarizes our attempt to excuse ourselves from making the effort, "Such knowledge is too wonderful for me; it is high, I cannot attain it." While forgetting that is is in climbing that we attain; it is in attempting that we follow; it is in striving that we fulfill God's expectations of us. "Let your light shine before men, that they may see your good works and give glory to your Father who is in heaven." We go from peak to peak.....

Let us consider the ways in which we are climbing from peak to peak.....even when we do not realize we are doing so.....

One of the first ways in which we climb is through experience. It's the most direct, most intensely personal method known for acquainting a person with facts. We've often heard it said "The proof is in the eating." There probably couldn't be a better illustration of experience than that....the actual confrontation of it! In progressive education the accent is upon experience. In the Francis W. Parker School of Chicago, one of the finest private schools in the country, teachers are encouraged to use this ingenuity in helping the students discover the world as it really is. One science teacher realizing she could talk all she wanted about farming and the dairy industry and her pupils still wouldn't really understand even a simplified experience for them by bringing a live cow to class in order to give them experience with dairying first hand! A little extreme perhaps, but they certainly understood where their glasses of milk came from!

Experience, then, is one of the first ways that we climb from peak to peak. But one other word should be mentioned about it before we go on to the second point. And that is the necessity to make a start. In mountain climbing there is no starting off the top; there is only the lure or the call of the top. And the process is the same for a Tientzing or a Hillary as it is for you and me. The only way to get to the top is by climbing from the bottom up. This may be hard to accept but there's no short-cut to the top. Experience has to be undergone…..lived through, accumulated before the heights of enterprise or uniqueness can be registered or the view really appreciated. There's no substitute for experience no matter how much we seek to avoid it!

Time magazine stated it well some time back concerning the future of space flights to the moon or Mars when it was observed when their assured, experienced captains guide the spacecraft into the velvet blackness, "They will be using manuals based on the flights and the mistakes of such early pioneers as Glenn and Carpenter."

"As we climb through experience and through each step forward it reveals the necessity of making new steps forward, unanticipated steps, towards a distinction one hadn't seen when one started out."

The second way in which we climb is in our relationship with one another. Look for a moment in the direction of Western Europe. Significant steps have been taken in international relations in the early sixties which point out the climbing nature of international contacts of the sort that would have been unthinkable and impossible even ten years earlier. While it was still too early to crow about the success of the Common Market becoming the third great power in the world, we cannot ignore the fact that the key to this door of enterprise already could be seen in any number of ways; from the movement of hundreds of thousands of workers and nationals from one country to another to live and work; in the abandonment of visas and immigration quotas between these countries; the removal of tariffs and import restrictions; the extensive use of automobiles, appliances, and a thousand and one articles not manufactured in the country in which they were sold. These are but a few of the signs of the times the tone can see in Europe today that are strong indicators that in these international relationships, old antagonists and embittered historical enemies can live and climb together toward the peaks of international peace and brotherhood where "Every step forward reveals the necessity of making new steps forward, unanticipated steps, towards a destination one hadn't seen when one set out."

Some years ago, the Paris daily Le Monde observed this international relationship very cleverly when it addressed itself to the possible entry of Britain into the Common Market and the mutual impact that each would make upon the other: "Britain is throwing off certain of the original traits to which she has always been so attached. She speaks of adopting the metric system. Automobiles there now have bright colors; the high buildings are going up in the middle of London, and worthy gentlemen no longer fear to walk about bareheaded." However the osmosis is not all in one direction. The whole Continent is now in the process of being conquered by one of the most agreeable British traditions, the weekend."

It's in our relationship that we really climb. We are forced off our status quo. We learn to do things we would never have done by ourselves. Have you ever stopped to think of how the relationship you've had with your wife or husband since marriage has produced a tremendous over-haul of your way of life? Thank of what you are doing today which would not have been possible if it hadn't been for your wife or husband's influence. I've heard it often from men who confess on rare occasions what their wives have done for them. "I've felt a great sense of inner peace, I've never known before. I'm not nearly so restless or as sloppy in my work habits as I once was. She's helped me immeasurably to value my time and talent in ways that I never dreamed were possible. I've been discovering new facets of her personality and mine that I never suspected were there!"

This is the height of discovery in human relationships, to learn that each helps another climb higher to become what each was meant to be in order to see that in our relationships with one another each step forward reveals the necessity of making new steps forward, unanticipated steps towards a destination which steps towards a destination one hadn't seen when one set out.

The final way in which we climb from peak to peak is by developing new thoughts and concepts of life. Let's consider for a moment what we've done thus far. We've recognized experience as the basic means by which to understand reality. This is simply the recognition of the facts of life. All of us have experience uniquely our own. Some of us should, perhaps, devote a little more time to it in terms of becoming acquainted with its necessity in order for any achievement being made. This is an intensely personal and private discovery that each of us must make.

Secondly, we've seen how through our relationships with one another there is a mutual interaction between us which helps each of us to climb; to reach heights we could never have attained by ourselves or through our own experience. Just think of the difference between Lindbergh's solitary flight over the Atlantic in 1927 and the space flights of Gagarin, Titov, Glenn and Carpenter in the early sixties and these flights if you wish a significant symbol of how dependent each of us is today upon one another and undoubtedly how very much more interdependent we shall become in the years ahead than we were in years past. This is the part of society or the community of which we are a part influencing us as well influencing others enabling all of us to rise to the heights of life improved.

The individual, then society, then the community of man and a whole range of concepts to which we pay lip-service but which do not really interest us very much because we do not understand their relationship to our daily lives. And yet, there should not be a conflict between what we believe and what we do.

The beatitudes have been called by numerous biblical scholars the ethics of impossibility and as if to excuse themselves at least trying to implement them in their lives, they dismiss them by calling them impractical, impossible, irrelevant to life. And yet is it not true that the Kingdom of God belongs to the humble-minded; that courage and comfort come to those who know what sorrow means; that the whole earth belongs to those who claim nothing for themselves; that those who seek to do goodness will be satisfied; that those who are merciful have mercy shown to them; that those who are utterly sincere will discover God; that those who make peace are the sons of God; that those who have suffered for the cause of goodness stand as the sentinels of God; That when you are blamed and falsely accused for the sake of truth you are in the noblest company of mankind sharing in the trials and tribulations of the best the world has ever seen or known! You are then sharing in the greatest tribute that can ever be paid to a person. He died that others may live as he lived and understand as he understood.

There are no easy concepts. There are no easy answers to life's questions. There are no thoughts that have ever been given final form. "Every time you get to the top of a peak, you see another peace in front of you.....a peak that you couldn't see from lower down. The ideal ends and recedes as you approach them; they're seen to be other and more remarkable than they seemed before the advance was begun. "Every step forward reveals the necessity of faking new steps forward, unanticipated steps, towards a destination one hadn't seen when one set out." We are constantly moving from peak to peak in our experience; in our relationships with others, in the formulation of new thoughts and concepts.

The Currents of Revolution

I t should be noted that I was part of a forty person graduate student committee selected by four different graduate organizations to participate in the first United States and Soviet Union exchange program in 1957. We were invited to travel to the Soviet Union from New York and spent two months traveling, interviewing, and witnessing events, visiting schools and universities across the Soviet Union for the first grand exchange program sponsored by both governments in an attempt in improve relations between our two countries. Hence this sermon which I'm in process of writing for my book entitled: "Sermons For The Separated" is hereby being included.

> "There is a tide in the affairs of men,
> Which, taken at the flood, leads on to fortune:
> Omitted, all the voyage of their life
> Is bound in shallows and in miseries.
> On such a full sea are we now afloat;
> And we must take the current when it comes,
> Or lose our ventures.

Not far from Nevsky Prospect and the Grand Palace of the former Czar of the Russian Empire, stands a statue put up in the late 19th century in honor of the last Czar, Nicholas !!. It was built so that it would face the huge Cathedral of St. Issac, the largest Cathedral of his Empire. He was a very devote man and this statue was to show his reverence for the church of which he was the head and the chief of all men in the Empire, divinely appointed head of Empire, and therefore, Church. On the base of the statue, in exquisite-bas-reliefs may be found various impressive scenes of his leadership, prominence, and power. There is one scene among many which hardly needs to be pointed out to the visitor, but by his guide, if he should happen to miss it. It shows the Lordly Monarch dismounting from his lavish, horse-drawn carriage as his poor, wretched subjects prostrate themselves before him on the ground in an act of obeisance to His Divine Majesty. The Communist guide waxes eloquently about the righteousness of the cause which finally did away with this form of exploitation and slavery of human beings and which would never be allowed to happen again in the Soviet Union! The revolution, you see, did away with these excesses of privilege and abuses of power.

If it were only true, for after you are there for a time you begin to realize that a new class has arisen in this allegedly classless society which is even more insidious than the last. It gives strong verbal agreement by means of slogans, posters, and charts to freedom, progress, and the social opportunity, while forming a bureaucratic elite of special privileges of housing, travel, and income for the Party members. Revolution resulted in the very evils the Communists deplored! While promising to abolish social differences, the Party must always increase them by acquiring the products of the nation's work-shops and granting privileges to its adherents. It must proclaim loudly its dogma that it is fulfilling its historical mission of "final" liberation of mankind from every misery and calamity while it acts in exactly the opposite way.

No, it's altogether too easy and plain to see what has resulted from the great day of the Revolution. Milovan Djilas, in his book "The New Class" portrays the noble spirit of the Communists on the opening of the great undertaking as he wrote,

"History does not have many movements that, like Communism, began their climb with such high moral principles and with such devoted, enthusiastic, and clever fighters, attached to each other not only by ideas and suffering, but also by selfless love, comradeship, solidarity, and that warm and direct sincerity that can be produced only by battles in which men are doomed either to win or die. Cooperative efforts, thoughts, and desires; even the most intense effort to attain the same method of thinking and feeling, the finding of personal happiness and the building of individuality through complete devotion to the party and workers' collective; enthusiastic sacrificing for others; care and protection of the young, and tender respect for the old-----these are the ideals of true Communists when the movement was in its inception and still truly Communist."

This was the movement when it was difficult to separate words from deeds. In this era of the Soviet Union, Communists believed in their ideals and aspired to put them into practice in their methods and in their personal life.

Djilas summed it up beautifully as he concluded "The world has seen few heroes as ready to sacrifice and suffer as the Communists were on the eve of and during their revolution. It has probably never seen such characterless wretches and stupid defenders of arid formulas as they became after attaining power. Honor, sincerity, sacrifice, and love of the truth were once things that could be understood for their own sakes; and now deliberate lies, slender, deception and provocation have gradually become the inevitable attendants of the new class."

Yes, the great day of this revolution never really came. The promises are still there. The hopes and aspirations have been whetted time and time again but government has induced and individually accepted privations for the long awaited day in which they would be fulfilled. The day in which the utopia would be reached! T. S. Elliot put is succinctly when he wrote:

"Between the idea
And the reality
Between the motion
And the act
Falls the shadow."

If we examine causes, if we undertake the task of looking at reasons why revolutions have occurred and are threatening in the world today (1957) we begin to see three factors that keep coming up again and again. First, there is a gross inequality of opportunity. The share of a nation's economic resources is unequally distributed so that a relatively few people of a nation reap the rewards of wealth while the majority continue in abject poverty and struggle to survive. This is the plight of approximately seventy percent of the world's peoples. If you want to visualize a contrast consider this: We in the United States, comprising roughly six percent of the world's population produce forty percent of the goods and services in the world.

Does this sound like a familiar theme? Does it seem that we still have yet to experience the real revolution? The total or radical change brought on by privations in which we are both guilty and guiltless; deprivers and deprived; exploiters and exploited; realists and idealists?

Having recently discussed three areas of Jesus life that made those who knew him to call him divine because of their experience of contact with him. We saw what he did, what he said, and what he was. But, did we also see that he was a revolutionist? That his concern, his message, and his life ws radically different from that of his compatriots? He was not interested in the status-quo. What he thought, believed and practiced was the very antithesis of conventionality. He was finally killed for the charge of being radical: a revolutionary! He wanted to bring each person to the fullest revelation of himself and this the leadership of the Jewish Community refused to do! They weren't ready for this final solution to the human problem.

Yet there is a revolution going on today. New nations are rising out of the ashes of old empires; newly independent peoples are searching for the meaning of their freedom; humankind is on the march for fairer distribution of their natural resources and equality of social and political opportunities to allow for each individual to find out his/her potentialities and bing them to their highest level of fulfillment in character and conduct. These are the goals of the present, on-going revolution. These are the aspirations of human kind;, the great theme of Jesus' life and message that character and conduct should become synonymous. And how may this be achieved? How may the search and searcher, the dream and dreamer; the deed and the man come closer together?

Consider these three passages that we heard earlier. First, "You are the light of the world…..Let your light so shine before men, that they may see your good works and give glory to your Father who is in heaven." Implied in this is a quality of being. So that when anyone looks at you they may be brought that much closer to God. What you do, say, and are is so similar to perfection that there is no fault to be found with you.

One of our professors at Seminary once told us of his visit to Gandhi. He represented a college magazine at the time. They talked for quite some time and before the professor left, he asked Gandhi if there was any particular message he had for him to take back to the youth of America. Gandhi declined to make any statement of that sort. He said he had nothing to say that would interest them. The professor was just going out of the gate when Gandhi called out, "Wait, you might tell them that my life is my message!"

In other words, what he said was "Let your light so shine before men that the darkness of despair, the fear of failure will be allayed and new dedication will ensue from your deeds.

Secondly, "As you did it to one of the least of these my brethren, you did it unto me."

Yes, and issue before us of the West is the creation under its leadership of a universal community in which free men make their own laws and live by them in peace. The essence of Western policy must be the construction of a universal order in which liberty under law becomes the right of all of humankind, not just that of the Western peoples exclusively." With these words, Robert Strausz-Hupe set forth the point at issue between Communism and ourselves which will spell the difference in the outcome of the present revolution through which we are all going.

Did you notice some of the words that he used? "A universal community.....Free men make their own laws and live by them in peace."

This is a political scientist talking, stressing what we need desperately to learn, that a revolution is going on and you and I have the power to bring about these results! We are agents of this revolution. We can set fire to the barriers keeping humankind in ignorance, poverty, and disease. A group of doctors have undertaken this attack by forming "Project Hope". a former Navy hospital ship will carry medical and nursing skills to underdeveloped nations of Southeast Asia this next year. It will be a floating medical center berthing in various Southeast Asian seaports making available over 400 beds, a staff of ten to fifteen doctors plus a 500 bed mobile hospital unit to be taken into the interior. Teams of five to seven physicians and two nurses will fly to these interior areas to give treatment and help train villagers in doctoring and nursing. At least one local physician is to be on hand with each team. In some of the areas the ship will serve, there is only one doctor for 80,000 patients. The reception of this project by doctors across the country has been amazing, according to Dr. William Walsh, head if this project. Several doctors have said they couldn't take four months off from their practices, but asked if they could be used for a month and they would pay their own expenses. This is service at its finest and no greater or more personal attack on the immediate problems of disease could be made! The revolution against one of humankind's prime enemies is thus being carried forward by willing hearts and able hands. And as Jesus said, "Let your light so shine before men that they may see your good works and glorify your father which art in heaven." The light of love and knowledge are being shed upon formerly hopeless thousands if not millions by this project. You and I have the power to revolutionize the world. We can be agents, we can be the means by which the message of brotherhood is heard throughout the world. We can exercise an influence by our community by being informed about what goes on in it, the nation and the world! We can suggest that humankind is of far more value than material; that human beings are children of God with potential as of yet unheard of and undreamed!

It is said of Saudi Arabia that civilization still lags centuries behind the West. "Filth and disease are endemic. Slaves are sold in the public squares along the El Has Coast. Thieves have their hands sliced off and the stumps immersed in boiling oil. Women found quietly of adultery are stoned to death. But the West doesn't mind. Ibn Saud has oil!" And Jesus said, "Even as ye have done it unto one of the least of these my brethren, ye have done it unto me." No, we don't want oil at any price! Who has been careless? Who it is that has taken oil from ore thought it more important than human dignity? Who has let slip the revolutionary opportunity to persuade this absolute despot to mend his ways and improve the terrible lot of his people?

Who of us is letting go of the opportunity of helping one of the least of these who's only glimpse of eternity may come through you?

A couple told me this past week that they were sorry but they couldn't come to church very much. "You see, in the fail we hunt, in the winter we ski, in the spring we fish, and in the summer, well, we play a lot of golf besides going on our vacation!" These are all worthy and healthy activities, but I wonder what they are playing in this revolution? What are they neglecting about themselves, to say nothing of what they aren't going for "The least of these"? Are they aware of the fact of what Shakespeare had one of this characters say in Julius Caesar.

> "There is a tide in the affairs of men,
> Which, taken at the flood, leads to fortune;
> Omitted, all the voyage of their life
> Is bound in shallows and in miseries.
> On such a full sea are we now afloat;
> And we must take the current when it serves,
> Or lose our ventures."

Are we losing opportunities that shall never come again? You and I have the power to revolutionize the world. We can be agents of this revolution. We can further the fuse of a universal community by giving voice to the unvoiced; by giving form to the unformed; by giving sight to the unseen by what we say, do and are.

As we heard previously when Gandhi was asked if he had a particular message for the youth of America his answer was, "Tell them for me, my life is my message!" As we said before, there's no greater affirmation to be made than that of what a person believes then by what he is and does. "Behold, the Kingdom of God is within you!" What you do for your neighbor when he/she is in difficulty is fulfilling a bit if the potential of the Kingdom. What you do and say to your son or daughter, father or mother can be the beginning of an experience of the Kingdom. How you look at your wife or husband, or what you say to her or him,, or what you do for each other will have no equal in feeling the Kingdom of God must be awfully close by if he or she is there! The Kingdom of God is within you, and you, and you!

The outcome of the revolution sweeping across the world with such swiftness and determination can only be won when we become agents influencing it in dedication to those principles of universal truth, brotherhood and liberty tempered by love without which it would ring with a hollow thud of premature success only to become the evil that it fought against. Our lives must become the message we profess if we are to achieve success in this mission to, for, and with humankind!

I Mean to Begin Again

When that great English painter of the 19th century, Burne-Jones was in his final years of life he was visited by an American woman who had done some painting. She considered herself quite a painter and made a big point about how the technique and ability of the artist was demonstrated in his paintings. She went on at great length telling this great artist about art and how painting was done and what she herself had done. Burne-Jones endured the lecture with great patience, and finally asked her if she cared to look at some of this paintings before she left. The woman graciously consented. He took her into his studio and she looked intently at his paintings. She was at least enough of an artist to recognize great art when she saw it and grew silent as she viewed painting after painting of this great artist. As they were saying good-bye to each other, Burne-Jones asked in a friendly voice, "And now, my dear, what do you mean to do with your art?" She bowed her head and replied quietly, "I mean to begin again."

Whenever we come in contact with someone great or some person who stands as a great contrast with what we have accomplished, or are, we can only say with the image of the contrast everlastingly before us….."I mean to begin again."

It's the sort of humbling experience all of us need on occasion to remind us of our many faults and limitations. It reminds us that no matter how well we've done or how highly we may think of ourselves, we still recognize we've a long way to go to perfection!

One of the reasons why we come to church each week is because we recognize our own imperfections and limitations. We realize that apart from God, we can do nothing which is meaningful or vital, but with his help and strength, we can overcome our handicaps. Our religion shows us what we can become while helping us to remember what we are. When we confront the life of Jesus, we see a portrait of what life can become. It also reminds us of what we are. We look at him and say, we mean to begin again.....

Each one of us needs to carry on this constant dialogue between what we are and what we can become. We look at him and see the love of God which allows us to begin again. Dr. Huston Smith, Professor of Philosophy and Comparative Religion at M. I. T. wrote in his book, "The Religions of Man" the only power that can effect transformations of guilt, fear, and self is love." It remained for our generation to discover that locked within the atom is the energy of the sun itself. For this energy to be released, the atom must be bombarded from without. So too there is, locked within every human life, a wealth of love and joy that partakes of God himself, but it too can be released only through external bombardment, in this care the bombardment of love. How true this is in the life of a child! No amount of threats or preaching can ever take the place of the parents' love in nurturing a loving and creative child. In psychology the discovery is likewise being made that love is a key term in theories of treatment. The love of God bombards us from without and thereby makes it possible for us to respond from within.

A young freshman just starting his first semester at a midwestern college came into the class of his favorite instructor one morning wondering how he had done on the paper he had written the previous week. It was his first paper and he hoped he had done well in it. He was somewhat afraid, however, as the instructor came into class bearing the armful of corrected themes. Had he gotten a passing grade? Had he demonstrated his respect for the high quality of study expected of him at this school? The instructor put the themes on his desk and opened the class by saying, "Last night I read some of the most significant words I have ever come across, and I want to share them with you." As he proceeded to read, the boy's heart leapt into his throat as he recognized his own words from the theme he had written the previous week. As the student related the incident later he said, "I didn't remember another thing that happened during the hour. But I shall never forget my feelings when I was brought to my senses by the closing bell. It was noon, and October was never so beautiful. I was exultant. If anyone had asked me for anything, I would have given it gladly, for I wanted nothing. I ached only to give to a world that had given so much to me."

This is the experience the disciples had through life, teachings, and demonstrated love of God that they experienced in Jesus. Because he melted the barriers of fear, guilt and self through this experience of love, it poured through them as if they were sluice gates, expanding the love they had felt for others until it embraced sinners and outcasts, Samaritans and enemies, not in order to receive it in return, but because this was its nature.

And so we came to another Communion service, carried on as a memorial of an ancient rite recalling the memory of Jesus as the personification of the love of God in human form. not standing in wrathful judgment of what we have done or have failed to do. Rather, as the one who stands and says quietly, "And what is it that you mean to do with your life?" we can only answer, "I mean to begin again!"

Crossroads

Dr. William Barclay, a great Scottish Biblical scholar, has written that ancient Rome maintained her empire through the occupation of strategic places such as road junctions from which whole areas could be controlled. Rome was accustomed to settle little bans of citizens usually composed of veterans of the army, who had served their time, and who had been granted citizenship. These colonies were the strategic centers which bound the Empire together. Here the Roman language was spoken; Roman dress was worn; the magistrates had Roman titles; Roman customs were followed; Roman law was observed and administered. These colonies were little bits of Rome in alien lands surrounded perhaps by barbarians, but controlling the countryside through their control of the crossroads of the world.

Paul saw the early church also as the church of the crossroads, establishing them in some of the major centers of the Roman Empire. Churches that were open to all peoples, embracing the world, yet decisively influencing the world around it for good. He pictured the strong bonds of fellowship and brotherhood as equivalent to those bonds of strength maintaining the Empire. Paul's churches were at the crossroads of decision.

This tendency to locate the church at the crossroads was carried on even through the dark and middle ages in Europe. The huge cathedrals or the little chapels were usually located at the crossroads, close to the stream of busy human life. Even in the development of our own country, the churches were located at the crossroads of commerce and trade; in the heart of the market-place where the thronging, surging masses of people and ideas could be reached. The trend that we have of the past decades has been a faulty one whereby new churches have been located in the suburbs on quiet, shady streets where neither the church nor its people cast much of an influence upon anyone, including themselves.

The church should stand at the crossroads as a symbol of its all encompassing influence upon life around it, participating in the joys and sorrows of all peoples as well as being the spokesman for an ever present God who is interested in each person doing his best to become what he was meant to be. To speak to the decisions that each person has to make concerning his future.

Crossroads, the church, then stands at the center of life as a symbol of choice; of decision which each person must make concerning his/her own life and the lives of their loved ones. Let us consider briefly what these crossroads are.

There is, first, the crossroad of identity. Who am I? What distinguishes me from others? What rights and privileges do I have? What are my assets as well as my liabilities? For every one of us there is this point of identity that has to be worked out. We never really seem to realize our identity. In fact, we find people who never seem to know who they are. They do not analyze the circles in which they live, and hence, can make no judgment about themselves. But each person starts from a particular core or center of life similar to every other- the core of the family. He/she is a member of it from birth. There are other persons in it with whom he/she learns to come to terms. They give him certain things while expecting others in return. There is a constant interaction going on between the other members of the family and himself/herself. Sociologists call this the socializing process. Through a give and take process of time and experience, a person begins to relate himself/herself to the others in this family through the various symbols of communication that he/she learns from those who teach him/her the rules of how to behave and when. The symbol of father and mother are two of the earliest that he/she learns to verbalize. Once he/she has established his/her identity in his/her family, he/she begins to do so with his/her community. He/she learns the boundaries of the streets; the places with open fields; the homes where other youngsters live; the location of the school and church; the places where the gang hangs out. He/she identifies himself/herself within the context of a community or a neighborhood.

Perhaps he/she experiences the crossroad of identity upon a wider realm as well. If he/she goes beyond the borders of his/her hometown or neighborhood he/she discovers he/she has yet another identity.....that of being a person of a particular nation; a member of a vast society of another country. He /she realizes that here is yet another identity beyond what he/she had ever known before. He/she may not want to head or really feel this identity, but if he/she forgets there are others who do not let him/her forget. Oversees you are an American. There is an identity here that calls forth privilege as well as responsibility.

The crossroads of identity then, is encountered as we learn the nature of the different groups in which we live. The interpersonal relationships of continuity between other people and ourselves is the way in which we find out who we are. Our identity is established as we discover the nature of the groups of which we are a part and see ourselves in relationship to these groups. We discover our identity as we discover our relationship to one another. "No man is an island, no man stands alone; Each man's joy is joy to me, Each man's grief is my own. We need one another. So I will defend, each man as my brother, each man is my friend." Ours is the choice then confirming our identity with the ever larger circles of which we are a part.

Another crossroad each one faces is the crossroad of meaning. Why am I here? What is the meaning of my existence? Each of us confronts these intensely personal questions at some point in life. A young student was grappling with this question of life's meaning over eighty years ago and found an newer. He was a student at Harvard and mulling intellectually all the whole range of thought wondering what life really meant. He was left with a heavy feeling of futility. One day he went into Appleton Chapel at Harvard University and wondered what it was all about. What is it all for, this toil and struggle? What is the good of it all? We've all sat down in this kind of a mood. And then, he wrote later in his autobiography, the thought came to me, "Life stands at the center of the world, human life. Whatever else may be doubtful, this at least is clear; whatever cleanses life, whatever redeems it from the power of evil, whatever gives it freedom, whatever brightens and glorifies it, that must be true because life is at the center of the world." And as George A Gordon came upon the implications of this meaning he realized that,

"Religion means insight, insight that generates power to overcome the world, the flesh and evil, insight that brings one humble but happy into the service of God." And thus having come to that arrangement of the chief values of life, this young man got up and went out of that chapel into fifty years of tremendous living and serving in the city of Boston as the minister of the old South Congregational Church.

The crossroads of meaning, can there ever be peace within our woulds unless we grapple with life and find its meaning? Unless we set a priority of values we shall not be able to discover the meaning within the variety of experiences that come upon us. So long as we find the renewing spirit of faith and hope within the lives of those who have suffered the ravages of life, so too, shall we find the meaning of life if we will but search for it.

The final crossroad at which we stand is the crossroad of purpose. Where am I going? What is the end toward which I am working? We usually find a person approaching this question as if he had no choice at all in the matter. He sort of lets himself be ordered wherever someone else leads. Several years ago a man came in for counseling who said he had lost his purpose in life. His wife had walked out on him with their two small children taking all their furniture and household goods leaving him nothing but the agony of memories he could not forget. He said his purpose was gone. There was no longer any reason in life for him. He wanted to give it up. It's hard to live with a purpose when you've made someone else your whole purpose in life. Dr. Walter Horton of Oberlin College once had his class write a paper on their belief in God. One girl wrote in her paper that she did not feel any need for believing in God because she was engaged to be married. She wrote, "My whole life revolves quite adequately astound the man I love." Professor Horton said he trembled for her because he knew the man, and while he was a nice guy, he lacked several important qualifications for the role of God! No human being can ever become the sole purpose of another, if for no other reason than that of impermanence.

I always feel sorry for the son or daughter who has given up his or her chances of marriage or a career because of feelings of obligation impressed upon them by an elderly parent whom they thought they had to care for, before any other consideration. Life always has a higher purpose than any single individual. We cannot make a God out of a person! For those of you who feel you simply could not live without that special him or her, may I remind you to remember no matter how much in love you may be, the end will always take him or her away from you!

The crossroad of purpose is not simply choosing the purposes we put into life, but also those which we discover in life because God put them there! These purposes are the ones we discover after certain doors have closed upon those rooms we had purposed to enter; the rooms of continuing good health; the rooms of continuing success; the rooms of continuing marital bliss, the doors to each of these rooms will one day close and the purposes for which we've lived and worked will be superseded by those of God.

In Edward R. Murrow's book, "This I Believe" written many years ago, he wrote of a great American actress who lost her young daughter. "When my daughter died of polio, everybody stretched out a hand to help me, but at first I couldn't seem to bear the touch of anything, even the love of friends; no support seemed strong enough.

"While Mary was still sick, I used to go early in the morning to a little church near the hospital to pray. I had rather cut God out of my life, and I didn't have the nerve at the time to ask Him to help me understand.....I kept looking for a revelation, but nothing happened.

"And then, much later, I discovered that it had happened, right there in the church. I could recall, vividly, one by one, the people I had seen there.....

"Here was my revelation. Suddenly I realized that I was one of them. In my need I gained strength from the knowledge that they too had needs, and I felt an interdependence with them....I experienced a flood of compassion for people. I was learning the meaning of 'Love thy neighbor.' " And thus did Helen Hayes learn that beyond her purpose was that of God waiting to be discovered.

Each one of us stands at continuing crossroads throughout our lifetimes-----crossroads calling for choice, our decision. God's purpose or ours? The crossroads of identity, meaning, and purpose, his or ours?

The Humility of Friendship

That great poet of the Victorian era, Robert Browning, in his poem, "Fears and Scruples" wrote "Hush, I pray you! What if this friend happens to be God?"

Dr. Leslie Weatherhead, in his book, the "Transforming Friendship" tells the story of a young woman who had just lost her husband after a short but fatal illness. It was the day after the funeral and he went to the young couples' home. As he came into the house he came into rooms that were still darkened. In one corner he saw an old white-haired woman sitting in a low chair, her face half hidden by her hand. Her other was on the shoulder of the young woman who had just lost her husband. She was sitting at the old woman's feet. It was a house filled with sorrow; the couple had only been married three months when the young man contracted pneumonia from which he never recovered. As Dr. Weatherhead came into the darkened room, the young woman turned almost ferociously upon him as he stood behind them both. "Where is God?" she demanded! "I've prayed to him? I've asked him to come and b e near me in my sorrow. Where is he? Away somewhere above the sky, or something? Why doesn't He come near me and make me know He is near? You preached once on "The Everlasting Arms. Where are they?" When the shower of tears and the storm of sobbing words had subsided Dr. Weatherhead did the only thing he knew he could do. He drew his finger-tips lightly down the older woman's arm and said, "They are here," he said. "They are around you even now. These are the arms of God....Where is He?" he asked. "Why doesn't He come near me?.....Hush, I pray you! What if this friend happens to be God?"

God speaks to us through the ministries of friendship; through the trust, the belief, the comfort, the love of another through friendship. We miss this obvious fact so often. We seem to think that God comes to us through some special revelation. We seem to feel he comes to us only through the overpowering strength of waves crashing against the cliffs and rocks of the shore. We know he comes to us through the ministry of overwhelming beauty in an evening sunset, or the intricacy and fragrance of a flower. But each day of our lives his presence is waiting for us to accept it, to experience it, to take it through the ministry of the friendship of other persons.

Do you have a wife who listens patiently to all of your wild plans for the future? Does she bear patiently all of the accumulated bitterness that builds up inside of you about that so and so of a boss or those shirkers who are only interested in how little they can do? Does she willingly participate with you in your dreams of what you're going to do even while you appear easily swayed from your purpose by other interests? Does she accept you openly without regard for your successes or your failures? Does she laugh with you on happy occasions and explore the depths of meaning with you in other experiences? Does the alchemy of her love soften the bitterness you feel when you've been greatly wronged or under the pressure of the strain and stress that builds up from trying to do too many things all at once? Then thank God for the humble privilege of knowing that God is so near to you, you can reach out to him through her! You think you only have a loyal wife and a trusting friend? "Hush, I pray you. What if this friend happens to be God?

I should like to talk to you this morning about the overwhelming, the humbling privilege we have of friendship. The humility of friendship whereby we can feel the presence of God close by. For you and I are so oblivious of what friendship can mean of what great ministry of God is performed through our ministry of friendship for one another. All of us recognize what friendship is, but few of us seem to know what it does.

One of the first things that friendship does is bring us close to God. When we try to imagine what God is like, we often have a very hard time of it. He is so great and vast that he becomes almost incomprehensible to us. But through friendship we are brought up to the very ends of God. I don't know how many of us have ever been at Jones Beach, or plum island of Bar Harbor and swam in the ocean. But if you were asked to describe what the Pacific, the Indian, the Atlantic oceans or any of the other seas and lakes were like, I'd bet you would have a hard time trying to describe what all of the water in the world is like to someone who has never seen an ocean or a great lake. But if you've seen it, bathed in it, sailed over it, watched it crash on the beach during a storm, you would quickly understand what an ocean is like because you've been touched, felt, experienced the near end of it wherever it was that you encountered it. And so it is with God. We come to the near end of God, to his presence, to an encounter with him through friendship. We know what he is like because we've experienced him through the friendship of another person.

God is mediated best in human form. This is the overwhelming truth of the incarnation theory of theology. That God was revealed to man in human form; in the life and example of a man called Jesus/. And what impressed the disciples, the rough fishermen, the crass tax-collector, the tough tradesmen of his day, was not so much what he said, or even what he did, so much as what he was. A completely loyal, trusting, understanding friend who was interested first and foremost in being a friend to those whose needs of loneliness, disappointment and frustration he knew so well.

Do you remember the story of Zacchaeus? Do you remember how as soon as Jesus came to his house he agreed to make amends for all the wrongs he had committed? It was nothing Jesus said to him. It was nothing Jesus did to him to persuade him to make amends for his wicked past. It was the simple extension to him of his friendship. And for the first time Zacchaeus felt touched as he had never been touched before. No one had ever been interested in him. No one had ever wanted to have anything to do with him. And yet, here was a man who wanted to extend his friendship to a friendless man. And Zacchaeus stood there and said "Here and now sir, I give half my possessions to charity, and if I have cheated anyone, I am ready to repay him four times over." And Zacchaeus had been touched by a friendship that brought him as close to God as he had ever come. And was Transformed by the contact.

Friendship brings us close to God. We can't help but feel the difference or express the difference visibly from what this closeness means in our lives.

The second affect of friendship is that through it we share in God. What was it Jesus said to his disciples about what each one could do to share in his work? "In as much as ye have done it unto one of the least of these, my brethren, ye have done it unto me." It sounds simple, but it's the extended hand of friendship through which we may share in total. It's not something so far distant or remote that we have to feel, it only happens to someone else. It couldn't happen to me! Think back over the times when you had a share in God through the friendship you extended to someone else. How about the time you took food over to a neighbor who was ill; or the looking after the children of the woman next door who had to take care of some business while you took care of her children; or the day your old neighbor died and you carried in a whole supper for the widow and saw to it that she didn't have to worry about her meals for those first few days alone, but invited her in to eat with you and help her get adjusted to the lonely days ahead.

Some time ago a woman had a rather sudden operation. There were four children in the family and while she was in the hospital her husband took care of the children over the weekends while during the week the children were taken care of by the neighbors. Food was brought in over the weekends. The husband was able to continue working with very little loss of time because of the ready and willing hands of friendship extended to him and his family in their critical hour of need! His neighbors shared in God with him and his family, as they shared in love what could not be shared in any other way.

In England they have had an organization for those in need called the Samaritan League. The League is exactly what the name implies......an organization dedicated to the doing of good towards their fellow human beings. A man, who is a member of this League, feels, when he has gone out to do a service for another human being in the name of Christ that he has not had an experience with that person, rather, he had had an experience with Christ. This is the real quality of the experience of friendship with another human being. We feel we've had a share in God.

In "My Lady of the Chimney Corner" there is an old woman who summarizes what I've been trying to say about sharing God through the common ordinary acts of friendship when she says: "God takes a han' wherever He can find it and just duz what He likes wi'it. Sometimes He takes a bishop's and lays it on a child's head in benediction, then He takes the han' of a doctor t' relieve pain; the han' of a mother t' guide her chile, an' sometimes He takes the han' of an oul craither like me t' give a bit comfort to a neighbor. But they're all ham's touch't be His Spirit, an' His Spirit is everywhere lukin' fur ham's to use."

And finally, through friendship we suffer with God. We experience what it means to be hurt; to bear the burden of a suffering heavenly Father. We feel the pain and the anguish that he feels when his children are abused or mistreated. This offering with God is the ultimate meaning of the cross, and friendship for Jesus means suffering with him.

Dr. Harry Emerson Fosdick once told of the terrible atrocities committed by the Turks against the Armenians during World War I. A certain Turkish officer took part in the looting and raiding of a certain Armenian home. The aged father and mother and the sons were taken out and shot in cold blood. The daughters were given away to the soldiery. The eldest girl was a girl of twenty. The officer kept her for himself. He used her for his own useful pleasure. By careful scheming she was at last able to escape to a camp where Arminian refugees were protected by the British. In common with other girls, she was given nursing training to make it possible for her to nurse her own countrymen and women who were sick. She did very well, and at length was moved to a hospital where Turkish prisoners were being nursed. She was put on night duty in the officers' ward. On the first night of her duty she passed down the ward with a hades lantern in her hand. Then a glint of light from her lantern flashed on a faces she recognized. She stopped, rooted to the ground in horror. She lifted the lantern to make assurance doubly sure. Yes, it could be no other! There lay the man who what wrought the ruin of her home, herself; the murder to her loved ones. He was dangerously ill. She confessed afterwards how bitter the struggle in her mind had been. But she nursed him back to health again until the doctors marveled at her care. When the Turkish officer recovered the doctor brought the nurse up to his bed and said to him, "But for this girl's devotion you should be dead." I think you have met before, the officer replied, white to the lips. "Yes," she said, "We have met before." When the doctor was out of hearing the officer almost hissed the words at her, "Why didn't you kill me?" And this was her answer: "Because cruelty cannot be righted by cruelty, nor violence buy violence. I am a follower of Him who said, "Love your enemies." That is my religion! The man lay silent for a long time, and then he spoke "I never knew there was such a religion," he said."If that is your religion tell me more about it, for I want it." Night after night for a few months she would come and tell him of the transforming love of men who suffered as God suffers for men.

Through the ultimate friendship of Jesus we suffer with God as he shares in the experiences, the suffering, and the cruelty of men towards one another."

Never Alone

It took a long time for it to happen, but it finally did. Three months after the decrees had been proclaimed by Caesar Augustus that a census should be taken of all the world, the order was sounded by crier throughout the towns and villages of the Roman Empire. All heads of households had to return to the town of their ancestors to register. Thus, Joseph of Nazareth, from the province of Galilea, set out for Bethlehem to the south in Judea. It was an eighty mile journey, but to travel with a pregnant wife on a donkey with few is any inns along the way was a major undertaking. It meant frequent stops and aching feet and sore muscles for the couple. And yet, who could quarrel with Roman authority at a time such as this. The law had been proclaimed and, therefore, it behooved all residents within the Empire to abide by it, irrespective of individual circumstances. The Roman law wasn't going to be held up because a baby was due.….After several days journey, quite likely having spent some nights sleeping under the stars, Joseph and his wife reached the ancestral town of Bethlehem. The pangs of birth were already upon Mary. She had felt them before, but not quite as persistent as this time. Joseph tried to make her comfortable while he looked for a place in which to stay. The inn was jam-packed with travelers and the inn keeper laughed out loud when Joseph told him his wife was about to bear a child and desperately needed a comfortable place to stay. He thought this fellow from up north was trying to play on his sympathies in order to get a room. But Joseph knew of Mary's needed and persisted in his request. The longer the inn-keeper listened, the more he realized this man wasn't trying to put one over on him but was deadly serious. He kept repeating the fact it was out of the question. There was simply no more room! But Joseph kept asking for just any place where she could have a little shelter; a little privacy; a little quiet place where she might bear her child.

Finally, the inn-keeper suggested the only place that he could think of where shelter, privacy and quiet existed was the stable! No one would be likely to disturb them there. And thus, Joseph brought Mary into the stable next to the inn in Bethlehem to give birth to her child.

Here they were, in a distant town, away from home, away from friends and family; away from sympathetic kinsman and understanding neighbors. What a time to have travelled! What a time to be away from home! What a time to have been all along in a strange town, where no one knew you and where you knew no one! Joseph and Mary must have felt quite alone and lonely. Even the inn-keeper, who at least knew the circumstances, didn't seem to concern himself too much with what was going on in his stable. He didn't go out to see of there was anything they needed or if there was anything he could do! The stable seemed a symbol of their loneliness. No one seemed to care; no one was interested in the agony and drama of the birth; no one was any different from the dumb animals in the stable who at least watched the drama unfold in dumb silence before them.

Joseph and Mary were so utterly, abjectly alone in the isolation of the town and stable! And yet, even while in the midst of this intense loneliness, the overwhelming affirmation of history has been the fact that their ordeal epitomized the eternal presence of God. They named their son Jesus, which meant "God with us" indicating their belief that God was with them even when no one else seemed to care.

There can be a tremendous meaning in the story of Christmas if we will but use a bit of creative imagination to visualize the scene. What does Christmas, the birth of Jesus, represent in light of this ancient setting? What does his birth mean today?

First, there is the reminder that birth is a momentous occasion. It's interesting that the shepherds would have been the first ones interested in seeing what had taken place in the stable. Luke described their interest in the 16th verse of the Second Chapter. "And they went with haste." In other words, they ran all the way from the hills on the outskirts of town into the town to the stable by the inn. There's a real excitement about a birth among shepherds. There was a constant appreciation of this fact in their lives. They witnessed the event hundreds of times as if for the first time to see the results. Birth was a momentous occasion to them.

I always feel sorry for the couple who feel there was nothing particularly spectacular about the birth of their child. Some people seem to take it so lightly, as if it held little consequence. On occasion I've found a husband did not have the time or maybe the interest to spend a few hours in a hospital waiting room until their child was born. Evidently little realizing what a momentous occasion birth was meant to be! It was Ralph Waldo Emerson who said it.

Birth comes as a perpetual Messiah to a fallen humankind, offering new hope, a new opportunity for correcting the mistakes of the past in the limitless possibilities of a new future represented within the life of a newly born child. A child is a bundle of possibilities of the future.

In the midst of this humble pathetic scene of a stable was reenacted a scene witnessed for thousands of years before and almost two thousand years since, but the rediscovery of the sacred meaning of birth as one of the greatest of human experiences is renewed by this scene in the manager of Bethlehem.

The second meaning this ancient story has is that even in Alaska there is light. What Luke doesn't say we've tried to say concerning the details of Jesus' birth. It was a dark bleak time for Joseph and Mary. All alone in a strange town. No one seemed to care that they were even there. Except for the shepherds, no one else seemed to have appeared. It was evidently too common for them. After all this was a rather simple couple unknown and unwelcome at this time in crowded Bethlehem. For the two of them, a dark time indeed. And yet into this darkness of indifference, callousness on the part of people who didn't care, and cruel disregard for the needs of a homeless couple, the light that lighted everyman was brought forth in the midst of this darkness which was to shine away the darkness of selfishness, cruelty, and strife among men. His light was to shine forth as the brilliant light of the world which could not be hid despite the darkness on the edge in which man stands.

The other meaning was a headline in the paper which read, "Christmas is for children." But Christmas is not only for children, it's for adults as well! It's a time for a glimpse of the light of love and good will to be seen among human beings. It's a time for actions to be witnessed that ordinarily would appear strange to some people. It's a time for giving our feelings a chance to show themselves without embarrassment. It's a time to say thank you to people by spending a few moments with them and by sharing in the excitement of acts of goodness that flow from the heart.

A few years ago, a couple of us were told that people look so strangely at him for being so friendly and always saying hello to each person he has met when he started a new job. But now at Christmas time the people he worked with seemed to do the same. They say hello and ask how things are going with that strange look. They can be friendly and interested in one another without embarrassment.

This is what Christmas does. This is what should prevail each day in human relationships. The darkness of indifference and despair should be swept away. Light is the power to dispel darkness. You have this power to move back the darkness in yourself and in others with the birth of light created when one illuminates another; when one heart kindles another; when one man strengthens another. Its flame also enlarges within you as you pass it on. Throughout history dictators, large and small, have tried to darken, diminish and separate men by force. But always in the end they fail. For always somewhere in the world the light remains; ready to burn its brightest where it is darkest.

And finally, his birth is an affirmation that God is always with us. This is what "Immanuel" means…..."God with us!" We are never alone. We are not left to curse the darkness, for in this event we have seen a great light. We have found that no matter how much a person, if forsaken or left alone, God is ever with us. We are never completely alone!

Prof. Donald F. Megnin, Ph.D.

That great Russian writer Leo Tolstoy wrote an overwhelming story three generations ago when he wrote, "Where love is, God." It's the story of an old cobbler by the name of Martin who was very much alone in the world. He sat reading a story about Christ and wished Christ would "visit him." He thinks about what he would do and what he would say if Christ should come to visit him today. He soon falls asleep and is startled by a voice which says, "Martin, Martin, look into the street tomorrow! I will come!" The old cobbler awakens and cannot make up his mind whether the voice was real or whether it was just a dream. The next day he found himself continually going to the window: "will he come, I wonder?" It is too much to expect, and yet such things have happened. During the day the old man brought in a sweeper from the street, gave him tea, and invited him to warm his hands by the stove. Then he brought in a soldier's wife when he saw from the window she was trying to wrap up her baby in a piece of old sacking, and he gave her food and drink and comfort. Then he brought into his little room an old woman selling apples and the boy who had run away with one of her apples. As he talks to her, her anger disappears, and, when they go, the boy is helping her to carry her load. The last scene shows Martin sitting at the table on which burns a solitary candle. The day is nearly over and He hasn't come. It must have been a dream after all. Yet, His voice seemed so real. But as the old man sits there, the figure of the snow-sweeper rises up before his eyes, and a voice says, Martin, Martin, do you not know me? This is I. Then the figure of the old apple-woman, and the Voice says, "And this also is I". And the great truth dawns upon the old cobbler that God has come near to him in each of these acts of kindness for his fellowmen. "Wherever love is, God is." He is always with us, no matter where we go or what happens to us. So long as we are able to recognize love, we find God with us. And this is what happened in that stable so long ago. The very atmosphere of the stable was transformed because love was there and wherever love is God is within the deepest darkness of a gleam of light.

We are never alone for there is ever within the most evil of circumstances the momentous occasion of the birth of new possibilities; within the deepest darkness a gleam of light; within even the loneliest of situations the truth that God is always with us waiting for us to recognize his presence so very close to us.

Printed in the United States
By Bookmasters